SATURDAY

IS

COOKOUTS

from kebabs and Ribs to Potato Salad and More

◆   ◆   ◆

TIME-LIFE BOOKS, ALEXANDRIA, VIRGINIA

TIME-LIFE BOOKS IS A DIVISION OF TIME LIFE INC.

TIME-LIFE CUSTOM PUBLISHING

Vice President and Publisher	Terry Newell
Project Manager	Jennifer Pearce
Director of Sales	Neil Levin
Director of New Product Development	Regina Hall
Managing Editor	Donia Ann Steele
Production Manager	Carolyn Mills Bounds
Quality Assurance Manager	Miriam P. Newton

Produced by Rebus, Inc.
New York, New York

Illustrations
William Neeper

Library of Congress Cataloging-in-Publication Data
Saturday is cookouts : from kebabs and ribs to potato salad and more /
from the editors of Time-Life Books.
p. cm. -- (The everyday cookbooks)
Includes index.
ISBN 0-7835-4788-9
ISBN 0-7835-4825-7
1. Barbecue cookery.   I. Time-Life Books.   II. Series.
TX840.B3S264   1996
641.5'78--dc20
95-51348
CIP

İntroduction

Cooking over an open fire is a way of life in many countries, and in America the backyard barbecue is a culinary tradition. We love the sensory delights and casual ease of grilling, but there are also some practical advantages to this ancient cooking technique. It is an easy way to get a delicious depth of flavor in the foods you prepare. Grilling is also a very versatile cooking method, ideal for a wide variety of foods. Close your eyes and inhale the aroma of *Sirloin Grilled in Garlic Smoke, Chicken Fajitas,* or *Tuna Steaks with Scallion-Yogurt Sauce.* And don't forget all the fixings, such as *Honey-Mustard Coleslaw* and *Roasted Herbed Potato Fans*! If you love great barbecue, you'll lick your lips over tangy condiments, spirited marinades, and kicky sauces like *Pineapple-Red Pepper Relish, Lemon-Pepper Marinade* and *Tomato-Molasses Barbecue Sauce.*

To help you enjoy Saturday at the grill, this book includes the following features:

- •All the recipes call for simple cooking techniques and ingredients easily available in the supermarket or pantry.
- •As a bonus, "Marinades and Sauces" can be used for more than just grilled foods. Try using them to "spice up" any of your own recipes, too.
- •Recipes labeled "Extra-Quick" take under 45 minutes to prepare. They are marked with this symbol: 🕐 (A full listing of these recipes is included in the index under the heading "Extra-Quick.")
- •In addition, there are many recipes that get fewer than 30 percent of their calories from fat. These recipes are labeled "Low-Fat" and are marked with this symbol: ♡ (A full listing of the low-fat recipes is included in the index under the heading "Low-Fat.")

Nowadays, barbecuing is not just a summer pastime but a frequent part of everyday eating. It is perfect for casual entertaining and brings ease and relaxation to any meal. Besides, you'll have *fun* cooking!

—*Mara Reid Rogers,*
author of numerous cookbooks and
spokesperson for The Everyday Cookbooks

Contents

SIDE DISHES

MARINADES AND SAUCES

INDEX

MEAT, POULTRY, AND FISH

BARBECUED SPARERIBS

SERVES 4

6 POUNDS SPARERIBS

3 GARLIC CLOVES, CHOPPED

1 MEDIUM ONION, COARSELY CHOPPED

3 POUNDS PLUM TOMATOES, COARSELY
   CHOPPED

1 STICK UNSALTED BUTTER

¼ TEASPOON CUMIN

½ TEASPOON CHILI POWDER

1 TABLESPOON CHOPPED PARSLEY

½ TEASPOON CAYENNE PEPPER

¾ TEASPOON BLACK PEPPER

1 TABLESPOON RED WINE VINEGAR

2 TABLESPOONS FRESH LEMON JUICE

ONE 6-OUNCE CAN TOMATO PASTE

⅓ CUP LIQUID BROWN SUGAR OR DARK
   CANE SYRUP

⅓ CUP DRY RED WINE

1. Prepare the grill.

2. Arrange the ribs in a single layer on the grill. Barbecue the ribs, turning often, for 20 minutes, or until the ribs lose their raw look.

3. Meanwhile, in a large saucepan, combine the garlic, onion, tomatoes, butter, cumin, chili powder, parsley, cayenne pepper, black pepper, vinegar, and lemon juice. Bring to a simmer over low heat; cover and cook, stirring occasionally, for 15 minutes.

4. Uncover the pan and add the tomato paste, liquid brown sugar or dark cane syrup, and wine. Return to a simmer and cook, stir-

ring, for 5 minutes, or until the mixture is thick and smooth. Remove from the heat.

5. Pour the sauce into a blender, 2 cups at a time, and blend until smooth, about 45 seconds. Transfer the sauce to a large mixing bowl. Repeat the process until all of the sauce has been puréed.

6. With a long-handled basting brush or wooden spoon, baste the ribs with barbecue sauce, turning frequently, until the ribs are crusty with sauce and have turned a dark brick-red color, another 25 minutes.

7. Transfer the ribs to a platter and serve.

Mexican Beef Skewers

SERVES 4

¼ CUP FINELY CHOPPED ONION

1 GARLIC CLOVE, CRUSHED

1 OR 2 RED CHILI PEPPERS, SEEDED
   AND FINELY CHOPPED

½ TEASPOON CUMIN

½ TABLESPOON CHOPPED FRESH
   OREGANO, OR ½ TEASPOON DRIED

½ TEASPOON PAPRIKA

1 TABLESPOON SESAME SEEDS

2 TABLESPOONS FINELY CHOPPED
   CILANTRO

1½ TABLESPOONS SAFFLOWER OIL

1 TABLESPOON FRESH LIME JUICE

2 BAY LEAVES

1¼ POUNDS ROUND STEAK, CUT INTO
   THIN STRIPS ABOUT 6 INCHES LONG

¼ TEASPOON SALT

1 LIME, CUT INTO 8 WEDGES

1. In a shallow dish or pie plate, combine the onion, garlic, chili peppers, cumin, oregano, paprika, sesame seeds, cilantro, oil, lime juice, and bay leaves.

2. Place the beef strips in the marinade and stir to coat. Cover the dish and let the meat marinate in the refrigerator for at least 4 hours, or overnight, turning it once or twice. Remove the steak from the refrigerator at least 30 minutes before cooking.

3. Prepare the grill.

4. Soak 8 wooden skewers in water for 10 minutes. Thread the strips of marinated meat onto the skewers, sprinkling them with any remaining marinade. Grill the skewers 4 to 5 inches from the heat, turning frequently, for 5 to 8 minutes.

5. Transfer the skewers to a serving platter and sprinkle with the salt. Serve the skewers garnished with the lime wedges.

PEPPER STEAKS FOR A CROWD

SERVES 16

1½ CUPS BEER

1½ CUPS CHILI SAUCE

2 ONIONS, COARSELY CHOPPED

½ CUP CHOPPED PARSLEY

⅓ CUP DIJON MUSTARD

3 TABLESPOONS BROWN SUGAR

2 TABLESPOONS WORCESTERSHIRE
SAUCE

2 TABLESPOONS PAPRIKA

1½ TEASPOONS DRY MUSTARD

½ TEASPOON BLACK PEPPER

SIX 1½-POUND T-BONE STEAKS
(1 INCH THICK)

⅓ CUP BLACK PEPPERCORNS

1. In a large glass baking dish, combine the beer, chili sauce, onions, parsley, mustard, sugar, Worcestershire sauce, paprika, dry mustard, and pepper. Place the steaks in the marinade, cover the dish with plastic wrap, and refrigerate for at least 4 hours or overnight, turning occasionally.

2. Prepare the grill.

3. In a mortar, or under the flat of a heavy knife blade, crush the peppercorns. Remove the steaks from the baking dish and discard the marinade. Sprinkle both sides of each steak with 1 tablespoon of the crushed peppercorns and press them into the meat with the heel of your hand. Place the steaks on the grill and cook them 4 inches from the heat for 9 to 10 minutes per side for medium-rare, or until desired doneness.

4. To serve, cut the meat from the bones and slice the steaks.

KITCHEN NOTE: *When you crush the peppercorns you'll notice their sharp, pungent aroma—which should convince you of the benefits of using freshly ground pepper for all your cooking. Pepper mills are inexpensive and can be kept on your table for everday use.*

STEAK WITH GLAZED SHALLOTS AND MUSHROOMS

SERVES 4

EXTRA-QUICK ♡ LOW-FAT

2 TEASPOONS SAFFLOWER OIL

½ POUND MUSHROOMS, HALVED IF LARGE

½ POUND SHALLOTS, PEELED

2 TABLESPOONS HONEY

1 TEASPOON CHOPPED FRESH TARRAGON, OR ½ TEASPOON DRIED

½ CUP MADEIRA OR PORT

½ CUP CHICKEN BROTH

2 TEASPOONS CORNSTARCH MIXED WITH 1 TABLESPOON OF THE BROTH

¼ TEASPOON SALT

¼ TEASPOON BLACK PEPPER

2 TOP LOIN STEAKS (ABOUT 1¼ POUNDS TOTAL), EACH CUT INTO 2 PIECES

1. Prepare the grill.

2. In a medium nonstick skillet, warm the oil over medium heat; add the mushrooms and sauté until lightly browned, about 4 minutes. Transfer the mushrooms to a bowl. Pour 1 cup of water into the skillet and add the shallots, honey, and tarragon. Partially cover the skillet; bring the liquid to a simmer and cook the mixture until the shallots are translucent, 8 to 10 minutes.

3. Return the mushrooms to the skillet and toss them with the shallots and the liquid until all are coated with a syrupy glaze, about 2 minutes. Keep warm.

4. In a small saucepan, reduce the Madeira or port by half over medium-high heat. Add the broth and bring the mixture to a simmer. Whisk the cornstarch mixture into the simmering liquid. Continue cooking the sauce until it thickens, and add ⅛ teaspoon of the salt and pepper. Keep the sauce warm.

5. Grill the steaks for 3 minutes on the first side. Turn the steaks over and season them with the remaining salt and pepper. Grill the steaks for 3 more minutes for medium-rare meat, or until desired doneness. Serve the steaks with the glazed shallots and mushrooms on the side and the sauce on top.

SIRLOIN GRILLED in GARLIC SMOKE

SERVES 6

EXTRA-QUICK

11 GARLIC CLOVES—10 CRUSHED, 1 FINELY CHOPPED

2 TABLESPOONS SAFFLOWER OIL

1 SMALL RED ONION, THINLY SLICED

1 TEASPOON FINELY CHOPPED FRESH GINGER

1 GREEN BELL PEPPER, CUT INTO THIN MATCHSTICKS

2 SCALLIONS, THINLY SLICED

2 TABLESPOONS RICE VINEGAR OR DISTILLED WHITE VINEGAR

¼ TEASPOON SUGAR

⅛ TEASPOON SALT

2 POUNDS BONELESS SIRLOIN STEAK (1½ INCHES THICK)

1. Prepare the grill. Place the crushed garlic cloves in 1 cup of cold water.

2. In a nonstick skillet, warm the oil over medium heat. Add the onion and cook, stirring frequently, until softened, 3 to 4 minutes. Add the chopped garlic and the ginger, and cook for 30 seconds; transfer to a bowl. Add the bell pepper, scallions, vinegar, sugar, and salt; stir and set aside.

3. Grill the steak for 7 minutes on the first side. Drain the water from the garlic cloves.

Remove the steak from the grill and toss the soaked garlic cloves directly onto the coals; a garlicky smoke will curl up. Return the steak to the grill and cook it on the second side for 5 to 7 minutes for medium-rare, or until desired doneness.

4. Transfer the steak to a platter and let it rest for 5 minutes. Carve the steak into thin slices; spread the onion-pepper relish over each portion just before serving, or present the relish on the side.

STEAK WITH RED PEPPER SAUCE

SERVES 4

1¼ POUNDS BEEF TENDERLOIN, CUT
  INTO 8 SMALL STEAKS
1 GARLIC CLOVE, FINELY CHOPPED
1 CUP RED WINE
½ CUP FRESH ROSEMARY SPRIGS, OR
  1½ TABLESPOONS DRIED
6 RED BELL PEPPERS

2 TEASPOONS RED WINE VINEGAR
¼ TEASPOON SALT
1 MEDIUM EGGPLANT, SLICED INTO
  8 ROUNDS
1 TABLESPOON OLIVE OIL
8 FRESH ROSEMARY SPRIGS, FOR
  GARNISH

1. Prepare the grill.

2. Put the steaks into a shallow dish large enough to hold them in a single layer. Sprinkle the garlic, wine, and rosemary over the steaks, and put them in the refrigerator to marinate, covered, for 2 hours.

3. About 1 hour before the steaks finish marinating, roast the peppers under a preheated broiler, turning them frequently until their skins blister, about 8 minutes. Transfer the peppers to a large bowl and cover the bowl with plastic wrap; the trapped steam will loosen the skins. When the peppers are cool enough to handle, peel, seed, and derib them over a sieve set in a bowl to catch the juices.

4. In a food processor or blender, purée the peppers with their juices. Add the vinegar and

salt to the purée. Pour the purée into a small saucepan and warm over medium-low heat while you prepare the eggplant and steaks.

5. With a paring knife, score both sides of each eggplant slice in a crosshatch pattern. Lightly brush both sides with the oil, then grill the slices until they are soft and browned, 2 to 3 minutes per side. Keep warm.

6. Take the steaks out of the marinade and pat them dry; discard the marinade. Grill the steaks for 4 minutes per side for medium-rare, or until desired doneness.

7. Divide the steaks and eggplant among 4 dinner plates. Spoon the warmed pepper sauce on top. Garnish each portion with the fresh rosemary, just before serving.

Top Loin Steaks with Sautéed Vegetables

SERVES 8

EXTRA-QUICK

2 TABLESPOONS OLIVE OIL

1½ TEASPOONS FENNEL SEEDS, LIGHTLY CRUSHED

3 GARLIC CLOVES, VERY THINLY SLICED

1 MEDIUM EGGPLANT, CUT INTO ½-INCH CUBES

1 CUP CHOPPED ONION

2 TABLESPOONS FRESH LEMON JUICE

1½ POUNDS TOMATOES, PEELED, SEEDED, AND CUT INTO ½-INCH PIECES

½ TEASPOON SALT

2 PINCHES OF BLACK PEPPER

4 TOP LOIN STEAKS (ABOUT 2¼ POUNDS TOTAL)

1. Prepare the grill.

2. In a large skillet, warm the oil over high heat. Add the fennel seeds and garlic, and cook them for 30 seconds, stirring constantly. Add the eggplant, onion, and lemon juice, and cook the vegetables for 5 minutes, stirring frequently. Add the tomatoes, ¼ teaspoon of the salt, and a pinch of pepper. Cook the vegetable mixture for 3 to 4 minutes, stirring constantly. Cover the skillet and set the mixture aside while you finish preparing the dish.

3. Grill the steaks for 3 to 4 minutes on the first side. Turn the steaks over and sprinkle them with the remaining ¼ teaspoon of salt and a pinch of pepper. Cook the steaks for an additional 3 to 4 minutes for medium-rare, or to desired doneness.

4. Let the steaks stand for 5 minutes before thinly slicing them against the grain. Divide the meat and vegetables among 8 dinner plates and serve at once.

PEPPERED STEAK ROLLS
WITH ONION COMPOTE

SERVES 4

♡ LOW-FAT

1¼ POUNDS WHITE BOILING ONIONS,
   BLANCHED IN BOILING WATER FOR 5
   MINUTES, DRAINED AND PEELED
½ CUP GOLDEN RAISINS
⅛ TEASPOON SALT
1 TEASPOON RED WINE VINEGAR

4 EYE ROUND STEAKS (ABOUT 1 POUND
   TOTAL)
¼ CUP GRAINY MUSTARD
¼ CUP FINELY CHOPPED PARSLEY
PINCH OF BLACK PEPPER

1. In a medium saucepan, combine the onions, raisins, salt, vinegar, and 1 cup of water. Bring the liquid to a boil, then reduce the heat and simmer the mixture until the onions are golden brown and the liquid has evaporated, 15 to 20 minutes.

2. Prepare the grill.

3. Place a steak on a work surface and steady it by pressing down with one hand. With a thin-bladed knife, halve the steak horizontally, stopping just short of the edge so that the 2 halves remain attached. Unfold the steak and place it on a square of plastic wrap. Cover with another piece of wrap and, with a meat mallet or rolling pin, pound the meat to ¼ inch. Repeat this process with the remaining steaks. Mix the mustard, parsley, and some pepper in a small bowl, and spread this mixture over the meat. Roll each steak into a loose bundle; tie the rolls with string to hold them together.

4. When the onions finish cooking, set them aside and keep them warm.

5. Grill the steak rolls for a total of 8 minutes, turning them every 2 minutes. Transfer the rolls to a platter; serve the onion compote on the side.

KITCHEN NOTE: *When you need to peel small boiling onions, blanching them makes them easier to peel and also tames their "bite" a little. You can also use this technique to loosen the skins of garlic cloves when you need to peel them in quantity.*

Beef Tenderloin Steaks with Roasted Garlic Sauce

SERVES 4

2 WHOLE GARLIC BULBS, CLOVES
SEPARATED BUT NOT PEELED
4 BEEF TENDERLOIN STEAKS (ABOUT 1
POUND TOTAL)
1 TEASPOON BLACK PEPPERCORNS,
CRUSHED

1 CUP RED WINE
3 SHALLOTS, SLICED OR ½ SMALL
ONION, FINELY CHOPPED
2 CUPS CHICKEN BROTH, PREFERABLY
REDUCED-SODIUM

1. Preheat the oven to 500°.

2. Scatter the garlic cloves in a small baking dish and roast them until they are very soft, 20 to 30 minutes. Set the garlic cloves aside to cool.

3. Prepare the grill.

4. Press the crushed peppercorns into both sides of each of the steaks and set them aside at room temperature.

5. Pour the wine into a small saucepan and add the shallots or onion. Boil the mixture over medium-high heat until nearly all of the liquid has evaporated, about 5 minutes. Add the broth, bring the liquid to a boil, and continue cooking it until it is reduced to about 1 cup, about 5 minutes.

6. Squeeze the garlic pulp from the skins into a food processor or a blender. Pour in the broth and purée the mixture. Put the garlic sauce (it will be thick) into the saucepan and keep it warm.

7. Grill the steaks for about 3 minutes on each side for medium-rare meat, or until desired doneness. Serve the steaks with the garlic sauce on top.

BEEF AND FRUIT KEBABS

SERVES 4

⏰ EXTRA-QUICK ♡ LOW-FAT

1 POUND LEAN BOTTOM ROUND, CUT
    INTO 1¼-INCH CUBES
¼ CUP DRY WHITE WINE
½ CUP APRICOT NECTAR
2 TABLESPOONS HONEY
2 TABLESPOONS FRESH LIME JUICE
1 TEASPOON GRATED LIME ZEST
1 GARLIC CLOVE, MINCED

1 TABLESPOON CHOPPED FRESH
    OREGANO, OR 1 TEASPOON DRIED
16 DRIED APRICOT HALVES
1 LARGE SWEET POTATO, PEELED AND
    CUT INTO 1-INCH CUBES
8 SMALL WHITE ONIONS, HALVED
2 SMALL ZUCCHINI, SLICED INTO
    1½-INCH ROUNDS

1. In a sturdy plastic bag, combine the beef, wine, nectar, honey, lime juice and zest, garlic, oregano, and apricots. Place the bag in the refrigerator and marinate several hours or overnight.

2. In a large pot of boiling water, cook the sweet potato and onions until fork tender, about 8 minutes.

3. Prepare the grill.

4. Alternately thread the beef, apricots, onions, sweet potatoes, and zucchini onto eight 12-inch skewers. Grill 8 inches from the heat for 12 to 15 minutes, brushing with the marinade and turning occasionally.

KITCHEN NOTE: *Skewers used for grilling should be long and flat; some have handles for easy turning. Skewers that are notched or twisted hold the food more securely. You can also get skewer rests or racks that keep the kebabs from rolling on the grill.*

GINGER-RUBBED STEAK

SERVES 6

EXTRA-QUICK

2 TEASPOONS CHOPPED FRESH GINGER
⅛ TEASPOON CAYENNE PEPPER

2¾ POUNDS BONELESS SIRLOIN STEAK
(1 INCH THICK)
¼ TEASPOON SALT

1. Prepare the grill. Using your hands, rub the ginger and cayenne pepper into both sides of the steak, and allow it to stand at room temperature for 30 minutes.

2. Cook the steak on the first side for 6 minutes, then turn it and sprinkle it with the salt.

Grill the steak on the second side for 5 to 6 minutes for medium-rare meat, or until desired doneness. Transfer the steak to a platter and let it rest for about 5 minutes before carving it into thin slices.

SWEET AFTERTHOUGHT: *Grilled tropical fruit is just the thing to follow this exotically spiced steak. Cut the leafy top from a ripe pineapple, then pare off the skin. Cut the pineapple crosswise into 1-inch-thick slices and grill them until hot and slightly browned. If you like, baste the pineapple slices with a mixture of melted butter, brown sugar, and cinnamon.*

SOUTH SEAS KEBABS

SERVES 4

♡ LOW-FAT

1 RIPE PAPAYA, PEELED, SEEDED, AND
  CUT INTO 1-INCH CUBES
1 POUND EYE ROUND, CUT INTO
  ¾-INCH CUBES
¾ CUP CHICKEN BROTH
1 SCALLION, TRIMMED AND THINLY
  SLICED
2 GARLIC CLOVES, FINELY CHOPPED
2 TABLESPOONS MINCED FRESH GINGER

1 TABLESPOON HONEY
¼ TEASPOON SALT
¼ TEASPOON CRACKED BLACK
  PEPPERCORNS
1 TABLESPOON CORNSTARCH MIXED
  WITH 1 TABLESPOON WATER
1 RED OR GREEN BELL PEPPER, CUT
  INTO ¾-INCH SQUARES

1. Purée about ⅓ of the papaya in a food processor or a blender; set the remaining cubes aside. In a shallow dish, mix the beef with the papaya purée; cover and marinate in the refrigerator for about 2 hours.

2. Prepare the grill.

3. In a small saucepan, combine the broth, scallion, garlic, ginger, honey, salt, and cracked peppercorns. Bring the mixture to a simmer over medium heat and cook for 3 to 4 minutes. Stir in the cornstarch mixture and continue cooking and stirring the glaze until it thickens, 1 to 2 minutes. Remove the glaze from the heat and set it aside.

4. Thread the cubes of beef, papaya, and bell pepper onto four 12-inch metal skewers. Grill the kebabs 4 to 5 inches from the heat for 3 minutes. Turn them and cook for 3 minutes more. Brush some glaze over the kebabs and cook them for 1 minute. Turn the kebabs again, brush them with the glaze, and cook for another minute.

5. Transfer the kebabs to a serving platter and brush them with the remaining glaze; serve the kebabs immediately.

CHILI BURGERS

SERVES 4

🕐 EXTRA-QUICK   ♡ LOW-FAT

1 POUND LEAN TOP ROUND BEEF, CUT
    INTO SMALL PIECES

¾ CUP CANNED KIDNEY BEANS,
    RINSED, DRAINED, AND MASHED

½ CUP FROZEN CORN KERNELS,
    THAWED

¾ CUP CHILI SAUCE

2 TABLESPOONS FINE UNSEASONED DRY
    BREAD CRUMBS

1 EGG WHITE

2 TEASPOONS CHILI POWDER

¾ TEASPOON CUMIN

½ TEASPOON OREGANO

½ TEASPOON SALT

4 HAMBURGER BUNS

1. In a food processor, process the beef until ground, about 30 seconds.

2. Prepare the grill. Spray the grill rack with nonstick cooking spray.

3. In a large bowl combine the beef, beans, corn, ½ cup of the chili sauce, the bread crumbs, egg white, chili powder, cumin, oregano, and salt. Shape into 4 burgers.

4. Grill the burgers, turning them as they cook, until cooked through, about 10 minutes. Grill the buns on the outer edges of the grill, cut side down, until lightly browned, about 30 seconds. Top each bun with a burger. Dividing evenly, spoon the remaining ¼ cup of chili sauce over the burgers and serve.

SUBSTITUTION: *Home-ground top round beef is even lower in fat than packaged lean ground beef, and the beans bulk up the beef mixture, letting you serve a bigger burger without adding fat. But the type of beans you use doesn't matter—pinto, black, or great northern beans will all work just as well as kidney beans.*

HAMBURGERS STUFFED WITH MONTEREY JACK

SERVES 4

⏰ EXTRA-QUICK

6 OUNCES MONTEREY JACK CHEESE

1½ POUNDS GROUND ROUND STEAK

¼ TEASPOON BLACK PEPPER

8 SLICES SOURDOUGH OR FRENCH
   BREAD

¼ TEASPOON SALT

1 GARLIC CLOVE, UNPEELED AND CUT
   IN HALF

4 SPINACH LEAVES

1. Prepare the grill.

2. Grate the cheese and shape into 4 slightly flattened balls, about the size of golf balls.

3. Divide the ground beef into 4 portions. Handling gently, press a ball of cheese into the center of each portion, making sure the cheese is surrounded by meat. Shape into patties and season both sides with the pepper.

4. Toast the bread on the grill on both sides and place on a heatproof platter in the oven to keep warm.

5. Grill the burgers for 6 minutes. Turn and sprinkle with the salt; grill for 4 minutes, or until cooked through.

6. Just before the burgers are done, remove the bread from the oven and rub a cut edge of an unpeeled garlic clove over 1 side of each slice. Place 1 slice, garlic-side up, on each plate. Top each with a hamburger, spinach leaf, and slice of bread.

MARINATED LONDON BROIL

SERVES 6

1 MEDIUM ONION, COARSELY CHOPPED
1 TABLESPOON GRATED LEMON ZEST
¼ CUP FRESH LEMON JUICE
½ CUP RED WINE VINEGAR
2 TABLESPOONS OLIVE OIL

2 TABLESPOONS DIJON MUSTARD
3 GARLIC CLOVES, MINCED
1½ TEASPOONS BASIL
½ TEASPOON BLACK PEPPER
1½ POUNDS LONDON BROIL

1. In a shallow baking dish big enough to hold the steak, combine the onion, lemon zest, lemon juice, vinegar, oil, mustard, garlic, basil, and pepper.

2. Place the steak in the dish and spoon some of the marinade over the top. Cover with plastic wrap and refrigerate for 8 hours or overnight, turning the steak every few hours.

3. Prepare the grill.

4. Remove the steak from the marinade and place on the grill. Broil 4 inches from the heat for 7 minutes.

5. Turn the steak over and broil for another 7 minutes for rare; 9 minutes for medium-rare; 11 minutes for medium to well done.

6. Let the steak stand for 5 minutes before carving into thin slices.

VARIATION: *The lemon-mustard-garlic marinade could serve as background for other herbs. Oregano would be a natural with the garlicky sauce; tarragon or rosemary would also make a very tasty marinade.*

SOUTHWESTERN BEEF SALAD

SERVES 4

🕐 EXTRA-QUICK ♡ LOW-FAT

¾ CUP TOMATO-VEGETABLE JUICE

¼ CUP FRESH LIME JUICE

1 TEASPOON OLIVE OIL

1 TABLESPOON TEQUILA (OPTIONAL)

2 TEASPOONS GROUND CORIANDER

1½ TEASPOONS CUMIN

¾ TEASPOON GRATED ORANGE ZEST

½ TEASPOON SALT

½ TEASPOON BLACK PEPPER

½ TEASPOON HOT PEPPER SAUCE

1 POUND FLANK STEAK

4 EARS OF CORN, HUSKS REMOVED

1 LARGE RED ONION, PEELED, HALVED, AND SLICED INTO ¼-INCH-THICK PIECES

8 PLUM TOMATOES, QUARTERED

3 CUPS BOSTON LETTUCE LEAVES

16 NONFAT TORTILLA CHIPS

1. Prepare the grill. Spray the grill rack with nonstick cooking spray.

2. In a large bowl, whisk together the tomato-vegetable juice, 1 tablespoon of the lime juice, and the oil; set aside. In a small bowl, stir together the remaining 3 tablespoons of lime juice, the tequila (if using), coriander, cumin, orange zest, salt, black pepper, and pepper sauce. Reserve 1 tablespoon of the mixture. Add the meat, turning to coat. Brush the reserved tablespoon of spice mixture onto the corn.

3. Place the meat and corn on the rack and grill, turning the meat and corn as they cook,

until the meat is cooked to medium-rare and the corn is lightly browned, about 8 minutes. As the meat and corn cook, place the onions and tomatoes on a grill topper and grill, turning as they cook until crisp-tender, about 5 minutes. Transfer the meat to a plate and transfer the vegetables to the bowl with the reserved tomato-vegetable juice mixture.

4. With a paring knife, scrape the corn from the cobs into the bowl. Thinly slice the beef and add to the bowl, along with any juices that have accumulated on the plate, and the lettuce. Stir to combine. Spoon the salad onto 4 plates and top with the tortilla chips.

Grilled Ham Steaks

SERVES 4

2 HAM STEAKS, WITH BONE (ABOUT 2 POUNDS TOTAL)

2 TABLESPOONS DRY MUSTARD

4 TEASPOONS BROWN SUGAR

ONE 7½-OUNCE CAN EVAPORATED MILK

PARSLEY SPRIGS, FOR GARNISH

1. Place the ham steaks in a shallow baking dish. In a small bowl, combine the mustard and brown sugar, and sprinkle it evenly over each steak. Pour the evaporated milk over the steaks and set aside until ready to grill.

2. Prepare the grill.

3. Place the ham steaks about 5 inches from the heat and grill until brown and bubbly, for 8 to 10 minutes, or until cooked through. Remove the ham steaks to a cutting board and slice each in half. Serve the ham steaks on individual plates, garnished with the parsley.

KITCHEN NOTES: *Ham steaks often curl when they're grilled or broiled. To avoid this, make several slashes in the fatty edges of the steak. You can also lightly score the top and bottom surfaces with a sharp knife, which helps the seasonings penetrate the meat as well.*

PIQUANT PORK SKEWERS

SERVES 6

¾ POUND PORK LOIN, CUT INTO 12 EQUAL STRIPS

1 GARLIC CLOVE, CRUSHED

2 TEASPOONS CORIANDER SEEDS, CRUSHED

¼ TEASPOON ALLSPICE

¼ TEASPOON PAPRIKA

2 TABLESPOONS SAFFLOWER OIL

⅓ CUP DRY RED WINE

¼ TEASPOON SALT

1 TABLESPOON LIGHT BROWN SUGAR

1. In a large, shallow dish combine the pork, garlic, coriander, allspice, paprika, and oil. Mix the ingredients together well, then cover the dish and let the meat marinate in the refrigerator for at least 1 hour and up to 24 hours.

2. Prepare the grill.

3. Thread each strip of meat onto a wooden skewer and lay the skewers on the grill. Using a plastic spatula, scrape down any marinade remaining in the shallow container and spread it on top of the skewers.

4. Grill the pork skewers for 6 minutes, or until they are lightly browned. Turn the skewers and cook for 5 minutes, or until cooked through.

5. In a small saucepan, combine the wine, salt, and sugar and cook over high heat until reduced to a syrupy glaze, 3 to 4 minutes. Drizzle the glaze over the pork skewers and serve.

PORK AND APPLE KEBABS

SERVES 4

1¼ CUPS BEER

6 BLACK PEPPERCORNS

½ TEASPOON GROUND CLOVES

2 TEASPOONS FINELY CHOPPED FRESH
SAGE, OR ½ TEASPOON DRIED

2 TEASPOONS CHOPPED FRESH
ROSEMARY, OR ½ TEASPOON DRIED

1 POUND PORK TENDERLOIN, CUT INTO
1-INCH CUBES

2 CRISP TART APPLES

1 TABLESPOON SAFFLOWER OIL

1. Pour the beer into a large bowl. Add the peppercorns, cloves, sage, and rosemary, and stir well. Add the pork cubes, turning them to coat evenly. Cover the pork and marinate in the refrigerator for at least 2 hours.

2. Prepare the grill.

3. Remove the cubes of pork from the marinade and reserve the marinade. Lightly oil 4 metal skewers. Core the apples and cut each one into 6 wedges; dip each piece of apple in the reserved marinade. Thread pieces of pork and apple alternately onto the skewers, starting and ending with a cube of pork. Stir the oil into the remaining marinade and baste the kebabs with this mixture.

4. Grill the kebabs 4 to 5 inches from the heat for 15 to 20 minutes, turning and basting several times, until cooked through.

KITCHEN NOTE: *If your skewers are round ones (formed from thick pieces of wire), double them up for a more secure grip on the food. Holding two skewers parallel, thread one piece of apple onto the pair to hold them steady. Then slide the remaining pork cubes and apple wedges onto the paired skewers.*

Skewers of Spiced Pork, Eggplant, and Pepper

SERVES 12

2 GREEN CHILI PEPPERS, FINELY
  CHOPPED
1 SMALL ONION, THINLY SLICED
ONE 2-INCH PIECE FRESH GINGER,
  MINCED
4 GARLIC CLOVES, CRUSHED
3 BAY LEAVES
1 LIME, GRATED ZEST AND JUICE
2 CINNAMON STICKS, HALVED
1 TABLESPOON WHOLE CLOVES
2 TEASPOONS CUMIN

¼ TEASPOON TURMERIC
½ TEASPOON SALT
PINCH OF BLACK PEPPER
⅔ CUP PLAIN LOW-FAT YOGURT
2 POUNDS PORK LOIN, CUT INTO
  ½-INCH SLICES
3 MEDIUM EGGPLANTS, QUARTERED
  AND CUT INTO 1-INCH SLICES
3 GREEN BELL PEPPERS, CUT INTO
  1-INCH SQUARES
1 TABLESPOON SAFFLOWER OIL

1. In a large bowl, combine the chili peppers, onion, ginger, garlic, bay leaves, lime zest and juice, cinnamon sticks, cloves, cumin, turmeric, salt, pepper, and yogurt. Add the pork slices, tossing them in the marinade to coat well. Cover the bowl and let the meat marinate in the refrigerator for 2 to 4 hours.

2. Prepare the grill. Spray the grill rack with nonstick cooking spray.

3. Remove the pork from the marinade and discard the bay leaves, cloves, and pieces of cinnamon sticks. Thread the pork onto 12 metal skewers. Thread the pieces of eggplant and bell pepper alternately onto 12 more metal skewers. Brush the vegetable kebabs with the safflower oil.

4. Grill the pork and vegetable kebabs 4 to 5 inches from the heat for 3 to 4 minutes on each side, until the meat is lightly browned and cooked through, and the bell peppers and eggplant are tender.

Hot-and-Spicy Pork Chops

SERVES 4

¼ CUP FRESH LIME JUICE

2 TEASPOONS HONEY

1 TEASPOON HOT PEPPER SAUCE

1 TABLESPOON RED WINE VINEGAR

¼ CUP UNSALTED TOMATO PASTE

1 TEASPOON ALLSPICE

PINCH OF BLACK PEPPER

4 PORK LOIN CHOPS (ABOUT
    1½ POUNDS TOTAL)

1. In a large bowl, combine the lime juice, honey, hot pepper sauce, vinegar, tomato paste, allspice, and pepper. Put the pork chops into the bowl and turn them to coat evenly with the marinade. Cover the bowl and refrigerate for 8 hours or overnight. Remove the bowl from the refrigerator about 1 hour before cooking time.

2. Prepare the grill. Spray the grill rack with nonstick cooking spray.

3. Grill the pork chops 4 to 5 inches from the heat for 6 minutes on each side, basting them with any remaining marinade. Transfer the pork chops to a platter and serve.

SWEET AFTERTHOUGHT: *While the coals are still hot, bake some bananas for dessert: Peel bananas and halve them lengthwise. Place two banana halves on a sheet of foil, sprinkle them with lemon juice and brown sugar, and dot with butter. Fold the foil into a packet and place on the grill; cook for 15 minutes, or until the bananas are hot and the sugar is melted.*

PORK TACOS

SERVES 4

⏰ EXTRA-QUICK ♡ LOW-FAT

ONE 4½-OUNCE CAN CHOPPED GREEN
CHILIES, DRAINED, JUICE RESERVED
¾ CUP CHOPPED CILANTRO
3 TABLESPOONS FRESH LIME JUICE
½ TEASPOON SALT
¼ TEASPOON GROUND GINGER
⅛ TEASPOON ALLSPICE
2 GARLIC CLOVES, MINCED
12 OUNCES LEAN PORK LOIN, TRIMMED
OF ALL VISIBLE FAT

1 MEDIUM RED ONION, HALVED AND
THICKLY SLICED
ONE 15-OUNCE CAN BLACK BEANS,
RINSED AND DRAINED
½ CUP CHOPPED TOMATOES
4 SCALLIONS, THINLY SLICED
8 FLOUR TORTILLAS
¼ CUP DICED AVOCADO
4 SPRIGS OF CILANTRO
4 LIME WEDGES

1. Prepare the grill. Spray the grill rack with nonstick cooking spray.

2. In a medium bowl, stir together the juice from the green chilies, the cilantro, lime juice, salt, ginger, and allspice. Remove 2 tablespoons and set aside.

3. Stir the garlic into the mixture in the bowl; add the pork and red onion, turning to coat. Place the pork on the grill and the onion on a grill topper and cook, turning the meat and onion until golden brown and cooked through, about 10 minutes. Transfer the pork to a cutting board and let rest 5 minutes before slicing.

4. Meanwhile, in a medium bowl, stir together the chopped green chilies, beans, tomatoes, scallions, and the reserved cilantro mixture. Spoon the bean mixture into the tortillas, add the meat and onion, and garnish with the avocado and cilantro sprigs. Serve with the lime wedges.

GARLIC AND ROSEMARY VEAL CHOPS

SERVES 4

⏰ EXTRA-QUICK

2 TABLESPOONS OLIVE OIL

1 TEASPOON GRATED LEMON ZEST

2 TABLESPOONS FRESH LEMON JUICE

2 LARGE GARLIC CLOVES, FINELY CHOPPED

3 SHALLOTS, FINELY CHOPPED

1 TABLESPOON CHOPPED PARSLEY

1 TEASPOON CHOPPED FRESH ROSEMARY, OR ½ TEASPOON DRIED

PINCH OF BLACK PEPPER

4 VEAL RIB CHOPS (ABOUT 2 POUNDS TOTAL), CUT BETWEEN THE BONES, ABOUT ½ INCH THICK

1 FENNEL BULB, CUT INTO THIN MATCHSTICKS

LEMON WEDGES, FOR GARNISH

1. Prepare the grill. Spray the grill rack with nonstick cooking spray.

2. In a small bowl, combine the oil, lemon zest, lemon juice, garlic, shallots, parsley, rosemary, and pepper. Arrange the veal chops side by side on the grill. Brush the tops with about a quarter of the lemon-shallot mixture and grill for about 3 minutes until golden brown. Turn the chops over and brush with another quarter of the lemon-shallot mixture. Grill for 3 minutes.

3. Mix the fennel into the remaining lemon-shallot mixture and spoon it on top of the chops. Press down lightly to smooth out any pieces of fennel that might be sticking up. Continue grilling for about 5 minutes, or until the fennel is golden brown.

4. Transfer the veal chops to a platter, garnish with the lemon wedges, and serve.

GRILLED VEAL CUTLETS

SERVES 4

8 SMALL VEAL CUTLETS (ABOUT
    ¾ POUND TOTAL)
¼ CUP PLAIN LOW-FAT YOGURT
1 TABLESPOON OLIVE OIL
1 TABLESPOON BALSAMIC VINEGAR

1 TABLESPOON GRAINY MUSTARD
PINCH OF WHITE PEPPER
8 FRESH SAGE LEAVES, FINELY CHOPPED
¼ TEASPOON SALT

1. Lay a cutlet on a work surface between 2 sheets of plastic wrap. Using the smooth side of a meat mallet or a rolling pin, pound it until it is about ⅛ inch thick. Repeat this process with the other cutlets.

2. In a small bowl, whisk together the yogurt, oil, vinegar, mustard, pepper, and sage. Brush the cutlets with the marinade and place them in a shallow dish; reserve any remaining marinade. Cover the dish and let marinate in the refrigerator for 4 hours or overnight. Remove the cutlets from the refrigerator 1 hour before you plan to cook them.

3. Prepare the grill.

4. Grill the veal cutlets 1 to 2 minutes on each side, basting them with any remaining marinade. Sprinkle the cooked cutlets with the salt and serve immediately.

KITCHEN NOTE: *Sage is one of Italy's favorite seasonings, and this recipe, with its veal, olive oil, and balsamic vinegar, is distinctly Italian. Gray-green sage leaves are long and narrow, with a velvety surface. If you are unable to buy fresh sage, use 1 teaspoon of crumbled dried sage.*

SWEET-AND-SPICY GRILLED LAMB

S E R V E S 4

♡ L O W - F A T

2 TABLESPOONS FRESH LEMON JUICE

2 TABLESPOONS LIGHT BROWN SUGAR

PINCH OF BLACK PEPPER

¼ TEASPOON ALLSPICE

¼ TEASPOON GROUND CLOVES

2½ POUNDS LAMB LOIN, BONED

1. Prepare the grill.

2. In a small bowl, combine the lemon juice, brown sugar, pepper, allspice, and cloves. Set the lamb loin in a shallow dish and pour the marinade over it, rubbing the spices into the meat. Let the meat marinate at room temperature for 1 hour, turning every 15 minutes.

3. Grill the lamb 4 to 5 inches from the heat for 5 minutes on each side, or until cooked through, brushing it occasionally with any remaining marinade. Let the lamb rest for 5 minutes before slicing it.

SWEET AFTERTHOUGHT: *For a low-fat version of a favorite summer dessert, make shortcakes with "yogurt cream" in place of whipped cream: Spoon nonfat vanilla yogurt into a cheesecloth-lined strainer placed over a bowl, then place in the refrigerator to drain for at least 2 hours. At serving time, lightly grill thick slices of low-fat pound cake (or angel food cake) and top them with the yogurt cream and your favorite berries.*

BARBECUED CHICKEN SANDWICHES

SERVES 4

EXTRA-QUICK   LOW-FAT

¾ CUP KETCHUP

2 SCALLIONS, CHOPPED

1 TABLESPOON WORCESTERSHIRE
   SAUCE

1 TABLESPOON MOLASSES

1 TEASPOON CUMIN

½ TEASPOON DRY MUSTARD

½ TEASPOON GROUND GINGER

2 TEASPOONS GRATED ORANGE ZEST

2 TEASPOONS OLIVE OIL

4 SKINLESS, BONELESS CHICKEN BREAST
   HALVES (ABOUT 1 POUND TOTAL),
   POUNDED ¼ INCH THICK

¼ CUP FRESH ORANGE JUICE

1 CUP FROZEN CORN KERNELS, THAWED

½ CUP FROZEN PEAS, THAWED

1 CUP CHERRY TOMATOES, HALVED

4 KAISER ROLLS, SPLIT

8 ROMAINE LETTUCE LEAVES

1. Prepare the grill.

2. In a medium saucepan, stir together the ketchup, scallions, Worcestershire sauce, molasses, cumin, mustard, ginger, orange zest, and oil over medium heat. Bring to a simmer and cook 3 minutes.

3. Place the chicken on the grill and brush with 2 tablespoons of the sauce. Grill the chicken 5 inches from the heat for about 4 minutes, or until the juices run clear when the chicken is pierced with a knife.

4. Add the orange juice, corn, and peas to the sauce and simmer for 2 minutes. Remove the sauce from the heat and let cool for 15 minutes. Stir in the tomatoes.

5. Line the kaiser rolls with the lettuce leaves, place the chicken on top, spoon the vegetable mixture over it, and serve.

CHICKEN FAJITAS

SERVES 4

¼ CUP COARSELY CHOPPED FRESH
    CILANTRO
3 TABLESPOONS OLIVE OIL
3 TABLESPOONS FRESH LIME JUICE
2 GARLIC CLOVES, MINCED
2 TO 3 TEASPOONS MINCED PICKLED
    JALAPEÑO PEPPER
¾ TEASPOON CUMIN
½ TEASPOON SALT

1 POUND SKINLESS, BONELESS CHICKEN
    BREAST HALVES
1 LARGE ONION, CUT INTO THICK
    SLICES AND RINGS SEPARATED
1 LARGE RED BELL PEPPER, CUT INTO
    ½-INCH-THICK STRIPS
1 LARGE GREEN BELL PEPPER, CUT INTO
    ½-INCH-THICK STRIPS
EIGHT 6-INCH FLOUR TORTILLAS

1. In a medium bowl, mix together the cilantro, oil, lime juice, garlic, jalapeño, cumin, and salt.

2. Put the chicken breasts on a large plate and spread 3 tablespoons of the marinade over both sides. Cover and refrigerate for 30 minutes. Add the onion rings and bell pepper strips to the remaining marinade in the bowl. Toss to mix, cover, and marinate 30 minutes at room temperature.

3. Prepare the grill.

4. Wrap the tortillas in foil and heat on the grill or in the oven, about 10 minutes. Remove from the heat and set aside.

5. Spread the vegetables on a grill screen, or put in a large skillet or baking pan on top of the grill, and cook 4 inches from the heat for 8 to 10 minutes, turning occasionally, until lightly charred and tender. Remove from the heat and keep warm.

6. Grill the chicken 4 inches from the heat for 8 to 10 minutes, turning once, until lightly browned and cooked through. Remove from the heat and cut into strips.

7. Fill the warm tortillas with some of the chicken and vegetables, roll up, and serve.

CHICKEN AND VEGETABLE KEBABS

SERVES 4

🕐 EXTRA-QUICK ♡ LOW-FAT

¾ TEASPOON OREGANO

½ TEASPOON ROSEMARY

¼ TEASPOON BLACK PEPPER

¼ TEASPOON GROUND ALLSPICE

½ TEASPOON SALT

1 POUND SKINLESS, BONELESS CHICKEN BREASTS, CUT INTO 2-INCH PIECES

1 RED BELL PEPPER, CUT INTO 2-INCH SQUARES

1 GREEN BELL PEPPER, CUT INTO 2-INCH SQUARES

1 RED ONION, CUT INTO 2-INCH WEDGES

ONE 8-OUNCE CAN NO-SALT-ADDED TOMATO SAUCE

½ TEASPOON GRATED ORANGE ZEST

1. Prepare the grill.

2. In a large bowl, combine ½ teaspoon of the oregano, the rosemary, pepper, allspice, and ¼ teaspoon of the salt. Add the chicken, bell peppers, and onion, toss to coat thoroughly, and let stand while you prepare the basting sauce.

3. In a small bowl, combine the tomato sauce, orange zest, the remaining ¼ teaspoon oregano, and remaining ¼ teaspoon salt, and stir to blend.

4. Alternately thread the chicken, bell peppers, and onion on 8 skewers. Brush the kebabs with some of the basting sauce and grill 5 inches from the heat for about 8 minutes, turning once halfway through cooking time and basting occasionally with the remaining sauce, or until the chicken is just cooked through. Place the kebabs on 4 plates and serve.

KITCHEN NOTE: *If you always have oranges in your kitchen, a recipe that calls for grated zest presents no problem. But if you seldom have oranges on hand, it's good to have a supply of zest at the ready. Buy a few oranges and grate the zest onto a small sheet of foil or plastic wrap; twist it closed and store in the freezer. Of course, this works with lemon and lime zest, too.*

LEMON CHICKEN KEBABS

SERVES 4

⏱ EXTRA-QUICK ♡ LOW-FAT

4 SKINLESS, BONELESS CHICKEN BREAST
HALVES (ABOUT 1 POUND TOTAL),
EACH CUT LENGTHWISE INTO
4 STRIPS

1 ZUCCHINI, CUT INTO ½-INCH-THICK
ROUNDS

1 RED BELL PEPPER, CUT INTO 1-INCH
SQUARES

¼ CUP FRESH LEMON JUICE

1½ TEASPOONS SUGAR

1 TEASPOON GRATED LEMON ZEST

¾ TEASPOON DRIED OREGANO

½ TEASPOON SALT

4 SMALL PITA BREADS, EACH CUT INTO
QUARTERS

1⅓ CUPS CHICKEN BROTH, PREFERABLY
REDUCED-SODIUM

2 GARLIC CLOVES, MINCED

½ TEASPOON GROUND GINGER

2 TEASPOONS CORNSTARCH

2 TABLESPOONS CHOPPED PARSLEY

1. Prepare the grill.

2. In a large bowl, combine the chicken, zucchini, bell pepper, 2 tablespoons of the lemon juice, the sugar, lemon zest, oregano, and ¼ teaspoon of the salt and toss to coat.

3. Alternately thread the zucchini, chicken, and bell pepper on 8 skewers. Grill the kebabs 5 inches from the heat for about 8 minutes, turning once halfway through cooking time, or until the chicken is just cooked through.

4. Wrap the pitas in foil, place on the grill with the chicken, and heat for 5 minutes, or until the pitas are warmed through.

5. Meanwhile, in a medium saucepan, combine the broth, remaining 2 tablespoons lemon juice, the garlic, ginger, and remaining ¼ teaspoon of salt. Bring to a boil over high heat and cook for 3 minutes. In a cup, combine the cornstarch and 1 tablespoon of water, stir to blend, and stir into the boiling broth. Cook, stirring constantly, until the sauce is slightly thickened, about 1 minute. Remove from the heat and stir in the parsley.

6. Place the chicken kebabs and the pitas on 4 plates and serve with the lemon sauce.

Cajun Chicken Kebabs

SERVES 4

⏱ EXTRA-QUICK

⅓ CUP WORCESTERSHIRE SAUCE

¼ CUP CIDER VINEGAR

⅓ CUP BROWN SUGAR

2 TABLESPOONS INSTANT COFFEE

¼ TEASPOON HOT PEPPER SAUCE

4 GARLIC CLOVES, MINCED

2 TEASPOONS BLACK PEPPER

2 TEASPOONS PAPRIKA

1 TEASPOON ROSEMARY

1 TEASPOON WHITE PEPPER

1½ TEASPOONS OREGANO

1½ TEASPOONS THYME

¼ TEASPOON CAYENNE PEPPER

½ TEASPOON SALT

2 BAY LEAVES

1 CUP KETCHUP

⅓ CUP VEGETABLE OIL

4 SKINLESS, BONELESS CHICKEN BREAST
HALVES (ABOUT 1¼ POUNDS
TOTAL), CUT INTO 1-INCH CUBES

2 MEDIUM RED ONIONS, CUT INTO
½-INCH-THICK WEDGES

1. In a medium saucepan, combine 1 cup of water with the Worcestershire sauce, vinegar, sugar, coffee, hot pepper sauce, garlic, black pepper, paprika, rosemary, white pepper, oregano, thyme, cayenne, salt, and the bay leaves. Stir in the ketchup and vegetable oil. Bring the mixture to a boil over medium-high heat, stirring frequently. Reduce the heat to low, cover, and simmer for 10 minutes.

2. Meanwhile, prepare the grill.

3. Alternating, thread the chicken and onion onto 8 skewers.

4. Pour half of the basting sauce into a bowl. Brush the kebabs with half of the remaining sauce and grill them 4 inches from the heat for 8 minutes. Turn the skewers over, brush with the remaining basting sauce, and grill until the chicken is cooked through, about 5 minutes.

5. Serve the kebabs with the remaining sauce on the side.

Hawaiian Chicken Kebabs

SERVES 4

⏰ EXTRA-QUICK ♡ LOW-FAT

ONE 7-OUNCE CAN PINEAPPLE
    WEDGES, DRAINED, JUICE RESERVED
¼ CUP KETCHUP
2 TABLESPOONS SOY SAUCE
2 TABLESPOONS LIGHT BROWN SUGAR
3 GARLIC CLOVES, MINCED
¼ TEASPOON RED PEPPER FLAKES

4 SKINLESS, BONELESS CHICKEN BREAST
    HALVES (ABOUT 1 POUND TOTAL),
    CUT INTO 4 PIECES EACH
1 LARGE RED ONION, CUT INTO
    1-INCH-THICK WEDGES
16 CHERRY TOMATOES

1. Prepare the grill.

2. In a large bowl, stir together ⅓ cup of the reserved pineapple juice, the ketchup, soy sauce, brown sugar, garlic, and red pepper flakes. Add the chicken and onion, stirring to coat.

3. Thread the chicken, pineapple, onion, and cherry tomatoes onto eight 10-inch skewers. Grill, turning the skewers and basting frequently with the juice, about 8 minutes, until the chicken and vegetables are cooked through.

Variation: *If you just can't get enough hot-and-spicy food, try substituting salsa-flavored ketchup for the regular ketchup in the marinade. Toss in an extra pinch of red pepper flakes or a few drops of hot pepper sauce, too, if you dare.*

CHICKEN TACO SALAD WITH SALSA DRESSING

SERVES 4

EXTRA-QUICK

1½ TEASPOONS CHILI POWDER

½ TEASPOON CUMIN

½ TEASPOON SALT

12 OUNCES SKINLESS, BONELESS
   CHICKEN BREAST HALVES

½ CUP SALSA

2 TABLESPOONS OLIVE OIL

2 TABLESPOONS FRESH LIME JUICE

3 CUPS TORN ICEBERG LETTUCE

2 CUPS BROKEN TORTILLA CHIPS

1 CUP SHREDDED SHARP CHEDDAR
   CHEESE

ONE 15-OUNCE CAN BLACK BEANS,
   RINSED AND DRAINED

ONE 11-OUNCE CAN CORN KERNELS,
   DRAINED

1 MEDIUM TOMATO, CUT INTO WEDGES

⅓ CUP THINLY SLICED RED ONION

1. Prepare the grill.

2. In a small bowl, combine the chili powder, cumin, and ¼ teaspoon of the salt. Rub the seasoning mixture on both sides of the chicken.

3. In a large salad bowl, mix together the salsa, oil, lime juice, and the remaining ¼ teaspoon salt. Set aside.

4. Grill the chicken 4 inches from the heat for 8 to 10 minutes, turning once, until cooked through. Transfer to a plate and let stand for a few minutes while assembling the salad.

5. To the dressing, add the lettuce, tortilla chips, cheese, black beans, corn, tomato, and onion. Cut the chicken into bite-size pieces and add to the salad. Toss to mix and serve.

CHICKEN DRUMSTICKS in BARBECUE SAUCE

SERVES 12

1 ONION, CHOPPED

1 CELERY RIB, DICED

1 GARLIC CLOVE, CRUSHED

TWO 14-OUNCE CANS NO-SALT-ADDED CHOPPED TOMATOES

3 TABLESPOONS DARK BROWN SUGAR

1 TABLESPOON WORCESTERSHIRE SAUCE

1 TEASPOON PAPRIKA

1 TEASPOON BLACK PEPPER

12 CHICKEN DRUMSTICKS (ABOUT 3½ POUNDS TOTAL)

1. In a large saucepan, combine the onion, celery, garlic, tomatoes, sugar, Worcestershire sauce, paprika, and pepper. Cover the pan and simmer the ingredients over low heat for 1 hour, or until the vegetables are very tender. Remove the pan from the heat. When the mixture has cooled, purée it in a food processor. Press the purée through a sieve into a clean pan; discarding the solids that remain in the sieve. Cook the sauce, uncovered, at a strong simmer, stirring occasionally, until it is thick and the quantity has reduced by half, about 30 minutes.

2. Prepare the grill. Spray the grill rack with nonstick cooking spray.

3. Brush the chicken drumsticks with some of the sauce and arrange them on the grill, 5 inches from the heat. Grill the drumsticks for 10 minutes, turning them frequently and basting with the sauce. Move the drumsticks to the outer edges of the rack and cook for another 10 to 15 minutes, turning and basting frequently, or until they are cooked through.

4. Pile the drumsticks on a serving platter and serve.

Yogurt-Marinated Chicken Thighs

SERVES 8

3 POUNDS CHICKEN THIGHS, SKINNED

½ TEASPOON SALT

¼ CUP FRESH LEMON JUICE

1 TABLESPOON GRATED LEMON ZEST

3 TABLESPOONS PAPRIKA

½ TEASPOON HOT PEPPER SAUCE

⅔ CUP PLAIN LOW-FAT YOGURT

1 TEASPOON BLACK PEPPER

8 CRISP LETTUCE LEAVES

1. Place the chicken thighs in a large, shallow baking dish. Cut 2 diagonal slits in opposite sides of each thigh.

2. In a small bowl, combine the salt, lemon juice, and lemon zest, then rub the mixture over each thigh and into the slits. Sprinkle 1 tablespoon of the paprika over the chicken thighs.

3. In another small bowl, mix together the hot pepper sauce, yogurt, and pepper. Using a brush, coat the paprika-sprinkled side of each thigh with the yogurt mixture. Turn the thighs over, sprinkle another tablespoon of paprika over them, and coat with the remaining yogurt mixture. Cover the chicken and refrigerate for 3 hours, or until the yogurt begins to dry.

4. Prepare the grill. Spray the grill rack with nonstick cooking spray.

5. Grill the thighs 5 inches from the heat for 10 to 15 minutes, turning them every 5 minutes. After the last turn, sprinkle the remaining paprika over the thighs. Serve the thighs immediately, garnished with the lettuce leaves.

KITCHEN NOTES: *Paprika and other red-pepper-based seasonings (such as chili powder and cayenne) lose their flavor somewhat more quickly than other spices; this process is speeded up in hot weather. If you've had a jar or tin of paprika on hand for more than a year, taste it to see whether it's lost its punch. The color is also a clue: If the color has faded, the flavor will be equally pallid.*

Citrus-Marinated Chicken

SERVES 4

2 LEMONS
1 ORANGE
¼ CUP MAPLE SYRUP
1 TABLESPOON OLIVE OIL

2 TEASPOONS THYME
½ TEASPOON BLACK PEPPER
2½ POUNDS CHICKEN PARTS

1. Grate the zest from the lemons and the orange. Squeeze the juice from the orange and the lemons; set the juices aside. In a small bowl, combine the grated lemon and orange zests and the maple syrup. Set aside until ready to cook the chicken.

2. In a shallow dish, thoroughly blend the reserved citrus juices, the oil, thyme, and pepper. Add the chicken and turn to coat completely. Cover the dish with plastic wrap and refrigerate. Marinate for at least 4 hours or overnight, turning the chicken every once in a while to marinate evenly.

3. Prepare the grill.

4. Brush the chicken parts with some of the marinade and arrange them on the grill, 5 inches from the heat. Grill the chicken for 15 to 20 minutes, turning frequently and basting with the sauce, or until the meat is cooked through.

CHICKEN WITH SPICY PEANUT SAUCE

SERVES 4

⏰ EXTRA-QUICK

6 QUARTER-SIZE SLICES FRESH GINGER, UNPEELED

2 GARLIC CLOVES, PEELED

4 MEDIUM SCALLIONS

5 TABLESPOONS SOY SAUCE

1 TABLESPOON ORIENTAL (DARK) SESAME OIL

4 SKINLESS, BONELESS CHICKEN BREAST HALVES (ABOUT 1¼ POUNDS TOTAL)

⅓ CUP CREAMY PEANUT BUTTER

¼ CUP CHICKEN BROTH

¼ TEASPOON RED PEPPER FLAKES

1 TEASPOON SUGAR

1. In a food processor, mince the ginger. Add the garlic and mince. Add the scallions and pulse on and off to finely chop.

2. In a large shallow dish, combine the minced ginger and scallions with 3 tablespoons of the soy sauce and the sesame oil. Add the chicken breasts and turn to coat them evenly with the marinade. Cover the dish with plastic wrap and set aside.

3. Prepare the grill.

4. In a small bowl, combine the peanut butter, broth, remaining 2 tablespoons soy sauce, the red pepper flakes, and sugar.

5. Reserving the marinade, remove the chicken and place it on the grill, 4 inches from the heat. Grill the chicken for 10 minutes, turn, and baste with the reserved marinade. Continue grilling for 8 to 10 minutes, or until the chicken is cooked through.

6. Transfer the chicken breasts to a platter, top with the peanut sauce, and serve.

TEX-MEX GRILLED CHICKEN

SERVES 4

⏱ EXTRA - QUICK   ♡ LOW - FAT

1½ CUPS MILD SALSA

2 TEASPOONS MILD TO MEDIUM CHILI
 POWDER

1 TEASPOON HONEY

1 TEASPOON GROUND CORIANDER

¾ TEASPOON CUMIN

½ CUP FROZEN CORN KERNELS

1 TABLESPOON FRESH LIME JUICE

4 SKINLESS, BONELESS CHICKEN BREAST
 HALVES (ABOUT 1 POUND TOTAL)

1. In a medium bowl stir together the salsa, chili powder, honey, coriander, and cumin. Remove 1 cup of the salsa mixture and set aside.

2. In a medium pot of boiling water blanch the corn for 30 seconds. Drain well and add to the bowl of salsa mixture along with the lime juice; set aside.

3. Combine the cup of salsa and the chicken in a shallow pan and marinate 20 minutes.

4. Prepare the grill.

5. Grill the chicken 6 inches from the heat for about 8 minutes per side, or until the chicken is cooked through. Serve with the salsa-corn mixture.

SWEET AFTERTHOUGHT: *Follow this spicy entrée with a sophisticated citrus dessert: Halve large navel oranges and loosen the segments with a grapefruit knife. Place the orange halves, skin-side down, on sheets of foil, then pour a spoonful of rum into the center of each orange half and drizzle with honey. Wrap and seal the orange halves in the foil. Place them (still cut-sides up) directly on the coals and cook for about 10 minutes, or until hot.*

LEMON-SAGE CHICKEN

SERVES 4

3 GARLIC CLOVES, MINCED

2 TEASPOONS GRATED LEMON ZEST

3 TABLESPOONS FRESH LEMON JUICE

1 TABLESPOON OLIVE OIL

1½ TEASPOONS SAGE

1 TEASPOON SALT

½ TEASPOON BLACK PEPPER

ONE 3- TO 3¼-POUND BROILER-FRYER, SPLIT

1. Prepare the grill.

2. In a small bowl, combine the garlic, lemon zest, lemon juice, oil, sage, salt, and pepper. Loosen the skin at the cut sides of each chicken half. Spoon some of the lemon-garlic mixture under the skin of each chicken half and spoon the remainder on the skin and the undersides of the chicken. Tuck the wings under. Wrap each half securely in heavy-duty foil.

3. Grill the foil-wrapped chicken 6 inches from the heat for 20 minutes. Unwrap the chicken carefully, reserving the juices. Place the chicken directly on the grill and cook for 15 to 20 minutes, turning often and basting with the reserved juices, until the chicken is well browned and cooked through.

TANGY BARBECUED CHICKEN AND BEANS

SERVES 4

🕐 EXTRA-QUICK ♡ LOW-FAT

1 LARGE ONION, FINELY CHOPPED

2 GARLIC CLOVES, MINCED

ONE 14½-OUNCE CAN NO-SALT-ADDED STEWED TOMATOES

⅓ CUP THAWED FROZEN ORANGE JUICE CONCENTRATE

3 TABLESPOONS CIDER VINEGAR

2 TABLESPOONS TOMATO PASTE

1 TABLESPOON MOLASSES

⅓ TEASPOON SALT

⅓ TEASPOON GRATED ORANGE ZEST

⅓ TEASPOON DRY MUSTARD

8 CHICKEN DRUMSTICKS (ABOUT 2 POUNDS TOTAL), SKINNED

ONE 19-OUNCE CAN RED KIDNEY BEANS, RINSED AND DRAINED

1. Prepare the grill. In a medium saucepan, combine 2 tablespoons of water with the onion, garlic, tomatoes, orange juice concentrate, vinegar, tomato paste, molasses, salt, orange zest, and mustard. Bring to a boil over medium-high heat, breaking up the tomatoes with the back of a spoon. Reduce the heat to low and simmer, stirring occasionally, until the barbecue sauce is slightly thickened, about 10 minutes.

2. Transfer 1½ cups of the barbecue sauce to a small bowl and brush the chicken gener-ously with this sauce. Arrange the chicken on the grill and cook 6 inches from the heat for about 15 minutes, turning and basting occasionally with the remaining sauce in the bowl, or until the chicken is just cooked through.

3. Stir the beans into the remaining barbecue sauce and cook until the beans are heated through, about 5 minutes. Place the chicken and the beans on a platter and serve.

BASIL-MARINATED CHICKEN

SERVES 4

¾ CUP MALT VINEGAR

½ CUP DRY WHITE WINE

2 LARGE SHALLOTS, THINLY SLICED

2 TEASPOONS MACE

⅛ TEASPOON BLACK PEPPER

2 TABLESPOONS CHOPPED FRESH BASIL,
OR 2 TEASPOONS DRIED

4 WHOLE CHICKEN LEGS (ABOUT 1¼
POUNDS TOTAL), SKINNED

¼ TEASPOON SALT

1. To prepare the marinade, combine the vinegar, wine, shallots, mace, pepper, and basil in a saucepan. Bring the mixture to a simmer over medium heat and cook for 2 minutes. Sprinkle the chicken legs with the salt and set them in a shallow baking dish. Pour the marinade over the chicken and cover the dish with plastic wrap. Refrigerate for 8 hours or overnight.

2. Prepare the grill.

3. Grill the chicken 4 inches from the heat for 8 minutes on each side, or until cooked through, basting several times during cooking. Transfer the chicken legs to a platter and serve.

SUBSTITUTION: *The heady spice called mace comes from the same plant as nutmeg: Mace is the delicate, lacy fiber that coats the nutmeg kernel. The thin layer of mace is peeled off and either ground or sold in small pieces called blades. Because the two spices are so closely related, nutmeg makes a satisfactory substitute for mace. Allspice is another possible replacement.*

CHICKEN AND VEGETABLE PACKETS

SERVES 4

2 TABLESPOONS OLIVE OIL

2 GARLIC BULBS

1 MEDIUM ZUCCHINI, CUT INTO ¼-INCH-THICK SLICES

2 SMALL GREEN BELL PEPPERS, CUT INTO ¼-INCH-THICK RINGS

4 LARGE RIPE TOMATOES, CUT INTO THIN WEDGES

1 CUP SLICED BLACK OLIVES

¼ TEASPOON SALT

⅛ TEASPOON BLACK PEPPER

2 TEASPOONS FENNEL SEEDS

8 SPRIGS FRESH THYME, OR 1 TEASPOON DRIED

EIGHT 2-INCH STRIPS OF ORANGE ZEST

4 SKINLESS, BONELESS CHICKEN BREAST HALVES (ABOUT 2 POUNDS TOTAL)

8 SPRIGS FRESH PARSLEY (OPTIONAL)

½ CUP DRY WHITE WINE

1. Prepare the grill.

2. Bring 3 cups of water to a boil in a small saucepan over medium heat. While the water is heating, spread ½ tablespoon of oil on each of four 18 x 12-inch sheets of foil, leaving a 1-inch border unoiled.

3. Separate the garlic into cloves, but do not peel. Add the garlic to the boiling water and cook for 2 to 3 minutes. Turn the garlic into a strainer and set aside.

4. Divide the zucchini among the foil sheets, arranging the slices in a single layer. Distribute half of the bell peppers, tomatoes, olives, and garlic over the zucchini. Season each portion with salt and pepper, sprinkle with half of the fennel seeds, and top each

with 2 sprigs of fresh thyme and 1 strip of orange zest. Layer each portion with 1 chicken breast and the remaining orange zest, bell peppers, tomatoes, olives, and garlic. Sprinkle with the remaining thyme and the parsley, if using, and drizzle with the wine.

5. Gather up the long ends of each foil sheet and fold over twice; fold up the short ends, forming packages, and place on the grill.

6. Cook the chicken 4 inches from the heat for 40 to 45 minutes, or until cooked through, depending on the thickness of the breasts.

7. Transfer the contents of each packet onto individual dinner plates. Pour any juices remaining in the foil over each portion and serve.

Grilled Chicken Caesar Salad

SERVES 4

EXTRA-QUICK

3 TABLESPOONS OLIVE OIL

3 GARLIC CLOVES—2 PEELED AND 1
   MINCED

1 TEASPOON GRATED LEMON ZEST

½ TEASPOON SALT

½ TEASPOON BLACK PEPPER

12 SLICES FRENCH BREAD

12 OUNCES SKINLESS, BONELESS
   CHICKEN BREAST HALVES

3 TABLESPOONS FRESH LEMON JUICE

6 TO 8 ANCHOVY FILLETS

2 TABLESPOONS MAYONNAISE

8 CUPS ROMAINE LETTUCE, TORN INTO
   BITE-SIZE PIECES

¼ CUP GRATED PARMESAN CHEESE

1. Prepare the grill.

2. In a small bowl, mix together 1 tablespoon of the oil, the minced garlic, lemon zest, and ¼ teaspoon each of salt and pepper. Lightly brush 1 side of each bread slice with a little of the oil mixture. Put the chicken on a plate and rub the remaining oil mixture over both sides. Set aside.

3. In a food processor, combine the lemon juice, anchovies, mayonnaise, and the remaining oil, salt, and pepper. With the machine running, drop the whole garlic cloves through the feed tube and process until puréed. Scrape the dressing into a large salad bowl.

4. Grill the chicken 4 inches from the heat for 8 to 10 minutes, turning once, until cooked through. Transfer to a clean plate.

5. Grill the bread about 1 minute, without turning, until toasted. Cut bread slices in half crosswise.

6. Mix the chicken juices that have collected on the plate into the dressing. Carve the chicken on an angle into thin strips. Add the Romaine and Parmesan to the dressing and toss to coat. Add the toast and chicken and toss again; serve immediately.

Honey-and-Soy-Glazed Chicken Breasts

SERVES 4

3 TABLESPOONS SOY SAUCE

2 TABLESPOONS MINCED SCALLIONS

1 TABLESPOON HONEY

1½ TEASPOONS GRATED FRESH GINGER

1 GARLIC CLOVE, MINCED

¼ TEASPOON RED PEPPER FLAKES

4 CHICKEN BREAST HALVES (ABOUT 2 POUNDS TOTAL), WITH SKIN AND BONE

1. In a small bowl, combine the soy sauce, scallions, honey, ginger, garlic, and red pepper flakes. Put the chicken in a baking dish and coat on both sides with the marinade. Cover and marinate in the refrigerator for 2 hours, or overnight.

2. Prepare the grill.

3. Grill the chicken 6 inches from the heat for about 20 minutes, turning often so it does not scorch, and brushing with any remaining marinade, until the chicken is a deep glazed brown and cooked through.

BUFFALO TURKEY STRIPS

SERVES 4

1 TABLESPOON OLIVE OIL

2 GARLIC CLOVES, MINCED

½ TEASPOON OREGANO

¼ TEASPOON SALT

¼ TEASPOON BLACK PEPPER

1 POUND TURKEY-BREAST CUTLETS,
CUT INTO 12 LONG STRIPS

4 TABLESPOONS UNSALTED BUTTER

1 TO 2 TABLESPOONS LOUISIANA-STYLE
HOT-PEPPER SAUCE

1 TABLESPOON MINCED SCALLIONS

1. In a medium bowl, stir together the oil, garlic, oregano, salt, and pepper. Add the turkey strips and toss to coat. Cover and marinate in the refrigerator for 1 hour. Soak twelve 10-inch wooden skewers in a pan of water while the turkey marinates.

2. Prepare the grill.

3. Thread a piece of turkey onto each skewer.

4. In a small saucepan, melt the butter with the hot-pepper sauce and scallions; remove from the heat and keep warm.

5. Grill the turkey skewers 4 inches from the heat, in batches if necessary, for 2 to 4 minutes per side, turning once, until lightly browned and cooked through. Spoon the sauce over the turkey, and serve.

HERBED TURKEY BURGERS

SERVES 4

⏲ EXTRA-QUICK

1 SMALL ONION

2 GARLIC CLOVES

¼ CUP (PACKED) PARSLEY SPRIGS

1 POUND GROUND TURKEY

½ CUP FINE UNSEASONED DRY BREAD
   CRUMBS

2 TABLESPOONS DIJON MUSTARD

2 TEASPOONS WORCESTERSHIRE SAUCE

1 EGG WHITE

1 TEASPOON OREGANO

¼ TEASPOON PEPPER

4 KAISER ROLLS, SLICED

4 TOMATO SLICES

4 ROMAINE LETTUCE LEAVES

1. Prepare the grill. Spray the grill rack with nonstick cooking spray.

2. In a food processor, mince the onion, garlic, and parsley.

3. In a medium bowl, combine the minced vegetables with the turkey, bread crumbs, mustard, Worcestershire sauce, egg white, oregano, and pepper, and mix to blend well.

4. Divide the mixture into 4 equal portions and form them into patties ½ inch thick.

5. Arrange the burgers on the grill and cook for 5 minutes on each side, or until cooked through.

6. Serve the turkey burgers on the kaiser rolls, topped with the tomato and lettuce.

SWEET AFTERTHOUGHT: *One barbecue classic deserves another, and "s'mores" are perfect after grilled burgers. Perhaps your scout-camping memories are a little hazy, so here's a refresher course: You'll need graham crackers, marshmallows, and chocolate bars. Toast a marshmallow over the fire, then sandwich it with a few squares of chocolate between 2 graham cracker squares.*

Lime-Grilled Turkey Cutlet Sandwiches

SERVES 4

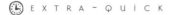 EXTRA-QUICK

4 TURKEY CUTLETS (ABOUT ½ POUND TOTAL), POUNDED ¼ INCH THICK

¼ CUP FRESH LIME JUICE

1 TABLESPOON OLIVE OR OTHER VEGETABLE OIL

½ TEASPOON SALT

¼ TEASPOON PEPPER

⅓ CUP MAYONNAISE

2 TABLESPOONS CHOPPED CILANTRO (OPTIONAL)

1 TEASPOON GRATED LIME ZEST (OPTIONAL)

1 SMALL AVOCADO

4 CLUB ROLLS OR OTHER HARD ROLLS

4 LETTUCE LEAVES

¼ CUP CRANBERRY SAUCE

1. Prepare the grill.

2. Place the turkey cutlets in a shallow dish and sprinkle them with 2 tablespoons of the lime juice, the olive oil, salt, and pepper. Turn the cutlets to coat them thoroughly with the seasonings.

3. Arrange the turkey cutlets on the grill and cook them 4 inches from the heat for 3 minutes per side, or until cooked through.

4. Meanwhile, in a small bowl, stir together 1 tablespoon of the lime juice, the mayonnaise, and the cilantro and lime zest (if using).

5. Slice the avocado and toss it with the remaining tablespoon of lime juice.

6. Split the rolls lengthwise and place them, cut-side up, on the outer edges of the grill for about 30 seconds, or until lightly toasted.

7. Spread both halves of each roll with the lime mayonnaise. Place a lettuce leaf and a turkey cutlet on half of each roll and top with avocado slices and a spoonful of cranberry sauce.

Grilled Turkey with Herb-Dijon Marinade

SERVES 8

♡ LOW-FAT

3 SCALLIONS, COARSELY CHOPPED

1 CUP PLAIN LOW-FAT YOGURT

¼ CUP FRESH LEMON JUICE

4 GARLIC CLOVES, MINCED

¼ CUP CHOPPED PARSLEY

1 TABLESPOON DIJON MUSTARD

2 TEASPOONS GRATED LEMON ZEST

2 TEASPOONS CUMIN

2 TEASPOONS GROUND CORIANDER

½ TEASPOON SALT

¼ TEASPOON BLACK PEPPER

¼ TEASPOON CAYENNE PEPPER

1 SKINLESS, BONELESS TURKEY BREAST
HALF (ABOUT 2¾ POUNDS)

1. In a medium bowl, combine the scallions, yogurt, lemon juice, garlic, parsley, mustard, lemon zest, cumin, coriander, salt, black pepper, and cayenne.

2. Slice the turkey across the grain into ¼-inch-thick scallops.

3. Add the turkey to the bowl and toss with the marinade. Cover the bowl and refrigerate for at least 3 hours, or overnight, tossing the turkey in the marinade occasionally.

4. Prepare the grill.

5. Arrange the turkey scallops in 1 layer on the grill. Cook the turkey 4 inches from the heat for 6 to 8 minutes on each side, or until golden and cooked through.

6. Transfer the turkey to a platter and serve.

Kitchen Note: *Turkey is so lean that it can easily dry out when grilled. If you grill the turkey straight from the refrigerator (rather than letting it come to room temperature) it will be less likely to overcook. Spoon any marinade left in the pan over the turkey when you first place it on the grill to help keep the meat moist.*

TURKEY CUTLETS WITH SAVORY FRUIT MARINADE

SERVES 4

⏱ EXTRA-QUICK ♡ LOW-FAT

1 ORANGE, PEELED AND COARSELY
  CHOPPED
4 SCALLIONS, COARSELY CHOPPED
2 GARLIC CLOVES, MINCED
2 TABLESPOONS CHOPPED PARSLEY
2 TABLESPOONS ORANGE MARMALADE
  OR APRICOT JAM

1 TABLESPOON OLIVE OR OTHER
  VEGETABLE OIL
½ TEASPOON SALT
¼ TEASPOON BLACK PEPPER
4 TURKEY CUTLETS (ABOUT 1 POUND
  TOTAL)

1. Prepare the grill. Spray the grill rack with nonstick cooking spray.

2. In a medium bowl, combine the orange and scallions. Stir in the garlic, parsley, marmalade or jam, oil, salt, and pepper.

3. Arrange the turkey cutlets on the grill and coat with half of the orange mixture. Grill the turkey 4 inches from the heat for 4 minutes, or until browned. Turn the turkey over and coat with the remaining orange mixture. Continue grilling for 4 minutes, or until the turkey is cooked through and the topping is golden.

4. Transfer the turkey to a platter and serve immediately.

CARIBBEAN CORNISH HENS

SERVES 4

TWO 1-POUND CORNISH HENS
2 TABLESPOONS DARK RUM
¼ CUP FRESH LIME JUICE
1½ TABLESPOONS HONEY

1 GARLIC CLOVE, CRUSHED
⅛ TEASPOON SALT
1 TABLESPOON CORIANDER SEEDS
½ TEASPOON BLACK PEPPERCORNS

1. With poultry or kitchen shears, remove the backbones from the hens by cutting along each side of the backbone until it is freed. Cut off and discard the leg tips and the tail. Wash the halves under running water and pat dry.

2. In a small bowl, mix together the rum, lime juice, honey, garlic, and salt. Place the hen halves in a shallow dish, just large enough to hold them. Rub the rum mixture over the hens, then set them aside in a cool place, covered, to marinate for 30 minutes.

3. Prepare the grill. Lightly oil the grill rack.

4. Using a mortar and pestle or a coffee grinder, coarsely crush the coriander seeds and peppercorns.

5. Arrange the hen halves on the grill and brush with some of the marinade. Press the crushed coriander seeds and peppercorns all over the skin-side of the hen halves.

6. Grill the hen halves 4 to 5 inches from the heat for 20 to 25 minutes, turning and basting every 5 minutes, or until the juices run clear when the meat is pierced with a knife.

Cornish Hens with Tarragon

SERVES 4

TWO 1½-POUND CORNISH HENS
1 STICK UNSALTED BUTTER, AT ROOM
   TEMPERATURE
1 TABLESPOON FRESH LEMON JUICE
1 TEASPOON MINCED GARLIC
½ TEASPOON SALT

⅛ TEASPOON BLACK PEPPER
2 TABLESPOONS CHOPPED FRESH
   TARRAGON, OR 1 TABLESPOON
   DRIED
2 TABLESPOONS CHOPPED PARSLEY

1. Prepare the grill. Spray the grill rack with nonstick cooking spray.

2. With poultry or kitchen shears, remove the backbones from the hens by cutting along each side of the backbone until it is freed. Place the hens on a work surface, skin-side up, spread open, and press the breastbone with the heel of your hand to flatten each hen.

3. In a small bowl, cream the butter with the lemon juice, garlic, salt, pepper, and tarragon. Brush both sides of the hens with some of the butter mixture.

4. Arrange the hens on the grill, skin-side down. Grill the hens 4 inches from the heat for 15 minutes, brushing with the butter mixture every 5 minutes. Use tongs to turn the hens, brush with more of the butter mixture, and grill another 10 to 15 minutes, or until the juices run clear when pierced with a knife.

5. Sprinkle the hens with the parsley; serve 1 half to each person.

TUNA STEAKS WITH
SCALLION-YOGURT SAUCE

SERVES 6

3 TUNA STEAKS (ABOUT 1½ POUNDS
   TOTAL)
8 SCALLIONS, CHOPPED
ONE 2-INCH PIECE FRESH GINGER,
   UNPEELED AND GRATED
4 GARLIC CLOVES
1 LARGE ONION, CHOPPED
¼ CUP FRESH LIME JUICE

¼ CUP WHITE WINE VINEGAR
2 TABLESPOONS OLIVE OIL
1 TEASPOON FINELY CRUSHED BLACK
   PEPPERCORNS
⅛ TEASPOON SALT
¾ CUP PLAIN LOW-FAT YOGURT
SLICES OF LIME, FOR GARNISH

1. Cut the tuna steaks in half and, if necessary, remove the bone from the middle of each steak. Place the fish pieces in a shallow dish.

2. In a food processor or blender, combine the scallions, ginger, garlic, and onion. Add the lime juice, vinegar, and oil, and process to a smooth purée. Stir in the peppercorns and salt.

3. Pour ⅔ of the mixture over the fish pieces, coating them evenly; reserve the remaining purée for use in the sauce. Cover the fish pieces and let them marinate in the refrigerator for at least 3 hours, or up to 12 hours. Remove the fish pieces from the refrigerator 1 hour before they are to be grilled.

4. Prepare the grill.

5. Soak 6 wooden skewers in water for 10 minutes. Thread 1 skewer through each piece of tuna about an inch from the straight, cut edge; this will keep the steak flat as it cooks. Grill the tuna 4 to 5 inches from the heat for 5 to 6 minutes, turn, and grill 5 to 6 minutes more, until lightly browned and cooked through.

6. While the tuna is grilling, in a serving bowl or sauceboat, combine the yogurt with the remaining scallion purée to make a sauce.

7. Transfer the tuna pieces to a heated platter and remove the skewers. Garnish the tuna with lime slices and serve the scallion-yogurt sauce on the side.

Tuna with Caper, Bell Pepper, and Pimiento Sauce

SERVES 6

6 TABLESPOONS UNSALTED BUTTER—4
  CUT INTO PIECES AND 2 MELTED
½ CUP FINELY CHOPPED ONION
1 TEASPOON FINELY CHOPPED GARLIC
½ CUP CLAM JUICE
¼ CUP FINELY CHOPPED GREEN BELL
  PEPPER
¼ CUP FINELY CHOPPED PIMIENTO
1 TABLESPOON DRAINED CAPERS
2 TEASPOONS TARRAGON VINEGAR

1½ TEASPOONS WORCESTERSHIRE
  SAUCE
¼ TEASPOON CAYENNE PEPPER
½ TEASPOON SALT
1 TABLESPOON FINELY CHOPPED
  PARSLEY, PREFERABLY FLAT-LEAF,
  PLUS ADDITIONAL SPRIGS, FOR
  GARNISH
6 TUNA STEAKS (¾ INCH THICK, ABOUT
  2 POUNDS TOTAL)

1. In a medium skillet, warm the 4 tablespoons of butter pieces over medium heat until melted. When the foam begins to subside, add the onion and garlic and cook, stirring frequently, until they are soft and translucent but not brown, about 5 minutes.

2. Add the clam juice, bell pepper, pimiento, capers, vinegar, Worcestershire sauce, cayenne pepper, and salt. Stirring constantly, bring to a boil over high heat. Reduce the heat to low and simmer the sauce, partially covered, until it thickens slightly, about 10 minutes.

3. Remove the skillet from the heat and stir in the chopped parsley. Cover the skillet and keep the sauce warm.

4. Prepare the grill.

5. Brush the tuna steaks on both sides with the 2 tablespoons melted butter. Grill the steaks about 5 inches from the heat, turning them, for 15 minutes, or until the flesh flakes easily when tested with a fork.

6. Transfer the fillets to a heated platter, garnish with the parsley sprigs, and pour the sauce over all. Serve at once.

Oriental Warm Grilled Tuna Salad

SERVES 4

⏰ EXTRA - QUICK

4 QUARTER-SIZE SLICES FRESH GINGER, CUT ¼ INCH THICK
2 GARLIC CLOVES
¼ CUP REDUCED-SODIUM SOY SAUCE
3 TABLESPOONS FRESH LIME JUICE
2 TABLESPOONS VEGETABLE OIL
1 TABLESPOON HONEY
1 TEASPOON GRATED LIME ZEST
¼ TEASPOON BLACK PEPPER

¼ TEASPOON RED PEPPER FLAKES
1¼ POUNDS TUNA STEAKS
4 CUPS SHREDDED NAPA OR CHINESE CABBAGE
4 CUPS SHREDDED RED LEAF LETTUCE
2 LARGE CARROTS, PEELED AND CUT INTO THIN MATCHSTICKS
2 CUPS BEAN SPROUTS
2 TABLESPOONS SESAME SEEDS

1. Prepare the grill. Spray the grill rack with nonstick cooking spray.

2. In a food processor, finely chop the ginger and garlic. Add the soy sauce, lime juice, oil, honey, lime zest, black pepper, and red pepper flakes and process to blend. Set aside half of the mixture to use as a salad dressing.

3. Brush the tuna steaks generously with some of the remaining ginger-garlic baste. Grill the tuna 4 inches from the heat for 5 minutes. Turn the fillets and brush with any remaining baste. Grill until the flesh is lightly colored and just flakes when tested with a fork, about 5 minutes.

4. Divide the cabbage, lettuce, carrots, and bean sprouts evenly among 4 dinner plates. Cut the grilled tuna into 1-inch chunks and place them on the salads. Pour the reserved salad dressing over all, then sprinkle with the sesame seeds. Serve while the tuna is still warm.

SWORDFISH IN APPLE-TARRAGON SAUCE

SERVES 4

 EXTRA-QUICK

2 TABLESPOONS VEGETABLE OIL

2 TABLESPOONS FINELY CHOPPED
SHALLOT

2 TABLESPOONS CHOPPED FRESH
TARRAGON, OR 2 TEASPOONS DRIED

½ CUP CLAM JUICE

¼ CUP UNSWEETENED APPLE JUICE

1½ TEASPOONS CORNSTARCH BLENDED
WITH 1 TABLESPOON COLD WATER

¼ TEASPOON SALT

2 PINCHES BLACK PEPPER

1½ POUNDS SWORDFISH STEAK, SHARK
STEAK, OR TUNA STEAK, CUT INTO 4
EQUAL PIECES

1 RED APPLE, QUARTERED, CORED, AND
CUT INTO THIN WEDGES

1 YELLOW APPLE, QUARTERED, CORED,
AND CUT INTO THIN WEDGES

1. Prepare the grill.

2. In a medium saucepan, warm 1 tablespoon of the oil over medium heat; add the shallot, and cook until it is translucent, 1 to 2 minutes. Add the tarragon, clam juice, apple juice, cornstarch mixture, ⅛ teaspoon of the salt, and a pinch of pepper. Whisking constantly, bring the mixture to a boil and let it thicken. Reduce the heat to low and simmer the sauce for 2 to 3 minutes; set the pan aside.

3. Season the fish steaks with the remaining ⅛ teaspoon salt and a pinch of pepper. Brush the steaks with the remaining oil. Grill the steaks 4 to 5 inches from the heat until the flesh is opaque when tested with the tip of a knife, 3 to 4 minutes per side.

4. While the steaks are grilling, reheat the sauce over low heat.

5. Transfer the swordfish steaks to a heated platter and pour the warm apple-tarragon sauce over them. Garnish the platter with the apple wedges and serve immediately.

Swordfish with Ancho Chili Sauce

SERVES 6

2 TABLESPOONS FRESH THYME LEAVES,
    OR 2 TEASPOONS DRIED
3 GARLIC CLOVES, FINELY CHOPPED
½ CUP FRESH LEMON JUICE
6 SWORDFISH STEAKS (½ TO ¾ INCH
    THICK, ABOUT 2 POUNDS TOTAL)
4 DRIED ANCHO CHILI PEPPERS,
    STEMMED AND SEEDED

1 OUNCE OIL-PACKED SUN-DRIED
    TOMATOES
¾ CUP CLAM JUICE
½ CUP PORT
2 TEASPOONS SAFFLOWER OIL

1. Prepare the grill. Spray the grill rack with nonstick cooking spray.

2. In a shallow dish large enough to hold the steaks in a single layer, combine the thyme, half of the garlic, and the lemon juice. Add the steaks and let them marinate, covered, in the refrigerator, turning them once or twice, for 1 hour.

3. In a heatproof bowl, cover the chilies with boiling water and let soak for 20 minutes.

4. Drain the chilies, discarding the water, and transfer them to a blender or food processor. Add the tomatoes and clam juice and purée the mixture.

5. In a small saucepan, bring the port to a boil over medium-high heat and cook it until it is reduced by half, 3 to 4 minutes. Stir in the chili-tomato purée and the remaining garlic. Reduce the heat to medium and cook the sauce, stirring occasionally, for 5 minutes. Strain the sauce through a fine sieve to cover the bottom of a heated platter.

6. Remove the swordfish steaks from the marinade and brush them with the oil. Grill the steaks 4 to 5 inches from the heat for 2 or 3 minutes per side, until the flesh is barely opaque when tested with the tip of a sharp knife. Arrange the steaks on the ancho chili sauce and serve immediately.

Swordfish and Vegetable Kebabs

SERVES 4

🕐 EXTRA-QUICK

2 TEASPOONS GRATED LIME ZEST

3 TABLESPOONS FRESH LIME JUICE

4 TABLESPOONS OLIVE OR OTHER
   VEGETABLE OIL

2 TABLESPOONS TOMATO PASTE

2 TEASPOONS DRY MUSTARD

4 GARLIC CLOVES, MINCED

¾ TEASPOON SALT

½ TEASPOON SUGAR

½ TEASPOON BLACK PEPPER

1 POUND SWORDFISH

1 LARGE RED ONION

1 LARGE YELLOW OR GREEN BELL
   PEPPER

8 CHERRY TOMATOES

1. Prepare the grill.

2. In a small bowl, combine the lime zest, lime juice, oil, tomato paste, dry mustard, garlic, salt, sugar, and pepper; set the basting mixture aside.

3. Cut the swordfish into 24 equal pieces. Cut the onion in half and then cut each half into quarters. Halve the bell pepper, seed and derib it, then cut it into 16 pieces, each about 1 inch square.

4. Dividing equally, and alternating, thread the swordfish, onion, bell pepper, and cherry tomatoes onto eight 10-inch metal skewers. Place the skewers on the grill and brush with half of the basting mixture. Grill the skewers 4 inches from the heat for 5 minutes. Turn them, brush with the remaining basting mixture, and grill until the fish is lightly colored, firm to the touch, and cooked through, about 5 minutes.

5. Arrange 2 skewers on each of 4 heated dinner plates and serve at once.

SWORDFISH WITH SPICY TROPICAL SAUCE

SERVES 4

⏰ EXTRA-QUICK ♡ LOW-FAT

1 ORANGE, PEELED AND COARSELY
   CHOPPED

1 SMALL RED ONION, COARSELY
   CHOPPED

2 TABLESPOONS CHOPPED SCALLION
   GREENS

ONE 8-OUNCE CAN CRUSHED
   PINEAPPLE, PACKED IN JUICE

3 TABLESPOONS TOMATO PASTE

3 GARLIC CLOVES, MINCED

2 TEASPOONS CORNSTARCH

¾ TEASPOON SUGAR

½ TEASPOON SALT

¼ TEASPOON RED PEPPER FLAKES

PINCH OF CAYENNE PEPPER

2 LARGE SWORDFISH STEAKS (1 INCH
   THICK, ABOUT 1½ POUNDS TOTAL),
   HALVED TO MAKE 4 EQUAL PIECES

2 TEASPOONS OLIVE OIL

1. Prepare the grill. Spray the grill rack with nonstick cooking spray.

2. In a medium saucepan, combine the orange, onion, scallion greens, pineapple and its juice, tomato paste, garlic, cornstarch, sugar, salt, red pepper flakes, and cayenne pepper. Bring the mixture to a boil over medium heat, stirring frequently, and cook, uncovered, stirring occasionally, for 10 minutes. Reduce the heat to low and simmer, uncovered, until thickened, about 10 minutes. Keep the sauce warm.

3. Brush the swordfish with the oil. Grill the swordfish steaks 4 inches from the heat for about 6 minutes on each side, or until lightly colored and the flesh just flakes when tested with a fork. Transfer the fish to a heated platter and pour the sauce over it.

KITCHEN NOTE: *When you spray the grill rack with nonstick cooking spray, keep it far from the fire, especially if you're using an aerosol: Sparks from the fire could cause the can to explode. You can also simply brush the grill with a small amount of vegetable oil.*

Swordfish with Lemon, Tomato, and Basil Sauce

SERVES 4

⏰ EXTRA-QUICK

3 TABLESPOONS DIJON MUSTARD

2 TABLESPOONS FRESH LEMON JUICE

2 TABLESPOONS OLIVE OIL

2 TABLESPOONS GRATED PARMESAN CHEESE

1 TEASPOON CHOPPED FRESH BASIL

¼ TEASPOON SALT

¼ TEASPOON BLACK PEPPER

4 SWORDFISH STEAKS (½ INCH THICK, ABOUT 2 POUNDS TOTAL)

1 SMALL TOMATO, COARSELY CHOPPED, PLUS 3 MEDIUM TOMATOES, THINLY SLICED

3 TABLESPOONS CHOPPED PARSLEY

1. Prepare the grill. Spray the grill rack with nonstick cooking spray.

2. In a small bowl, stir together the mustard, lemon juice, oil, Parmesan, basil, salt, and pepper.

3. Place the swordfish steaks on the grill and brush them lightly with some of the basil basting sauce. Grill the steaks 4 inches from the heat until opaque on top, 3 to 4 minutes.

4. Meanwhile, add the chopped tomato and the parsley to the remaining basting sauce.

5. Turn the swordfish steaks and spoon the tomato-basil basting sauce over them. Grill until the fish is lightly colored, firm to the touch, and just flakes when tested with a fork, 3 to 4 minutes.

6. Arrange the sliced tomatoes on a platter and top them with the grilled swordfish steaks. Spoon any remaining sauce over the steaks and serve immediately.

BAY-SCENTED
SKEWERED SWORDFISH

SERVES 4

1 SMALL ONION, CUT INTO ¼-INCH
   SLICES AND SEPARATED INTO RINGS
¼ CUP FRESH LEMON JUICE
4 TEASPOONS OLIVE OIL
½ TEASPOON SALT

½ TEASPOON BLACK PEPPER
1½ POUNDS SWORDFISH STEAK, CUT
   INTO 1-INCH CUBES
20 LARGE BAY LEAVES

1. In a deep bowl, combine the onion, 2 tablespoons of the lemon juice, 2 teaspoons of the oil, the salt, and pepper. Add the swordfish cubes, turning them to coat well. Cover and let the fish marinate in the refrigerator for 2 to 4 hours, turning it occasionally.

2. In a heatproof bowl, cover the bay leaves with 2 cups of boiling water and let them soak for 1 hour to prevent them from burning when grilled.

3. Prepare the grill. Spray the grill rack with nonstick cooking spray.

4. Drain the bay leaves and remove the swordfish cubes from the marinade. Thread the fish and bay leaves, alternating them, on four 10-inch metal skewers, pressing the pieces firmly together.

5. Combine the remaining 2 tablespoons lemon juice and 2 teaspoons oil and brush the lemon oil evenly over the fish.

6. Grill the skewers 4 to 5 inches from the heat, turning them every minute or so, until the fish is lightly colored and evenly cooked through, 6 to 7 minutes. Transfer the skewers to a heated platter and serve immediately. Discard the bay leaves.

COD WITH TOMATO AND BELL PEPPER RELISH

SERVES 4

⏱ EXTRA - QUICK

4 MEDIUM PLUM TOMATOES

1 SMALL RED BELL PEPPER

3 SCALLIONS

¼ CUP FRESH BASIL LEAVES OR
1½ TEASPOONS DRIED

2 TABLESPOONS OLIVE OIL

2 TABLESPOONS RED WINE VINEGAR OR
CIDER VINEGAR

½ TEASPOON BLACK PEPPER

¼ TEASPOON SALT

4 COD OR HALIBUT STEAKS (¾ INCH
THICK, ABOUT 1 POUND TOTAL)

1. Prepare the grill. Spray the grill rack with nonstick cooking spray.

2. Coarsely chop the tomatoes and place in a bowl. In a food processor, coarsely chop the bell pepper, scallions, and basil. Transfer the vegetable mixture to the bowl with the tomatoes and stir in the oil, vinegar, pepper, and salt until well combined. Strain the excess liquid from the tomato and bell pepper relish into a small bowl. Set the relish aside.

3. Place the cod steaks on the grill and brush them with some of the relish liquid. Grill the steaks 4 to 5 inches from the heat for 4 minutes, turn them, and brush with some more of the liquid. Grill the steaks until they are lightly colored, and the flesh just flakes when tested with a fork, about 4 minutes more. Transfer the fish steaks to a heated platter and top each of them with some of the tomato and bell pepper relish.

SOLE FILLETS WITH SHALLOT-GINGER GLAZE

SERVES 4

⏱ EXTRA-QUICK

4 SOLE FILLETS OR OTHER FIRM-
FLESHED WHITE FISH (ABOUT
1½ POUNDS TOTAL)

3 TABLESPOONS UNSALTED BUTTER

6 SHALLOTS OR 1 MEDIUM ONION,
MINCED

4 QUARTER-SIZE SLICES FRESH GINGER,
MINCED

1 GARLIC CLOVE, MINCED

½ CUP CHICKEN BROTH

4 TEASPOONS CORNSTARCH

⅓ CUP DRY WHITE WINE

1 TABLESPOON FRESH LEMON JUICE

2 TEASPOONS GRATED LEMON ZEST

¼ TEASPOON BLACK PEPPER

1. Prepare the grill. Spray a grilling basket with nonstick cooking spray and arrange the sole fillets in the basket.

2. In a small skillet, warm the butter over medium-high heat until melted. Add the shallots, ginger, and garlic and cook, stirring, until the mixture is just golden, 8 to 10 minutes. Remove the skillet from the heat.

3. Brush each of the sole fillets with half of the shallot-ginger mixture and close the basket. Grill the fillets 4 to 5 inches from the heat, turning them once, until lightly colored and the flesh just flakes when tested with a fork, about 6 minutes.

4. Meanwhile, in a small bowl, blend together the chicken broth and cornstarch.

5. Return the skillet to medium heat and stir in the wine, lemon juice, lemon zest, and pepper. Bring to a boil, add the cornstarch mixture, and cook, stirring constantly. Reduce the heat to medium-low and simmer, stirring occasionally, for 1 minute, or until thickened and slightly glossy.

6. Arrange the sole fillets on a heated platter and drizzle the shallot-ginger glaze over them. Serve immediately.

SOLE WITH CUCUMBER-DILL SAUCE

SERVES 4

⏲ EXTRA-QUICK ♡ LOW-FAT

1 TABLESPOON UNSALTED BUTTER,
   MELTED

¼ CUP (PACKED) FRESH DILL SPRIGS OR
   1½ TEASPOONS DRIED

½ TEASPOON SALT

½ TEASPOON BLACK PEPPER

1 CUP PLAIN LOW-FAT YOGURT

3 TABLESPOONS FRESH LEMON JUICE

2 TEASPOONS GRATED LEMON ZEST

½ TEASPOON DRY MUSTARD

ONE 2-INCH PIECE OF CUCUMBER,
   PEELED, SEEDED, AND FINELY
   CHOPPED

¼ CUP FINELY CHOPPED RED BELL
   PEPPER

4 SMALL SOLE FILLETS OR OTHER FIRM-
   FLESHED WHITE FISH (ABOUT
   1½ POUNDS TOTAL)

1. Prepare the grill. Spray a grilling basket with nonstick cooking spray.

2. In a small bowl, combine the melted butter with 1 tablespoon of the fresh dill (or ½ teaspoon of the dried), ¼ teaspoon of the salt, and ¼ teaspoon of the pepper.

3. In a serving bowl, combine the yogurt, lemon juice and zest, mustard, the remaining 3 tablespoons fresh dill (or 1 teaspoon dried), the remaining ¼ teaspoon each of salt and pepper. Stir in the cucumber and bell pepper.

4. Brush the dill butter over the sole fillets and arrange them in the grilling basket; close the basket. Grill the fillets 4 to 5 inches from the heat, turning them once and brushing them with the dill butter again, until the fish just flakes when tested with a fork, about 7 minutes. Divide the sole fillets among 4 heated plates and top each with a generous dollop of cucumber-dill sauce.

KITCHEN NOTE: *If you use a wire grill rack, fragile fish fillets are likely to stick to it and break. A grilling basket sprayed with nonstick cooking spray holds the fillets securely and lets you turn them all at once, without resorting to tongs or a spatula.*

GRiLLED TUПA WiTH CHiLi BARBECUE SAUCE

SERVES 4

4 TUNA STEAKS (ABOUT 1½ POUNDS
  TOTAL)
¼ CUP CHOPPED CANNED GREEN
  CHILIES, DRAINED

3 TABLESPOONS SOY SAUCE
1 TABLESPOON OLIVE OIL
1 GARLIC CLOVE, MINCED
¼ CUP CHILI SAUCE

1. Place the tuna in a shallow dish. In a small bowl, mix the chilies, soy sauce, olive oil, and garlic. Spoon ¼ cup of the mixture over the tuna steaks, turning to coat both sides. Cover and marinate in the refrigerator for 1 hour.

2. Mix the remaining soy sauce mixture with the chili sauce. Cover and refrigerate until ready to use.

3. Prepare the grill.

4. Remove the steaks from the marinade. Grill for 6 to 8 minutes, turning once, or until the fish is just opaque in the thickest part. Serve with the sauce.

Monkfish Skewers with Lime Butter

SERVES 4

 EXTRA-QUICK

1 STICK UNSALTED BUTTER, CUT INTO PIECES

2 SMALL GARLIC CLOVES, MINCED

2 TABLESPOONS FRESH LIME JUICE

½ TEASPOON SALT

1 SMALL BUNCH OF CILANTRO, MINCED

3 LIMES, QUARTERED LENGTHWISE

2 POUNDS MONKFISH, CUT INTO 2-INCH CHUNKS (ABOUT 24 PIECES)

2 TEASPOONS GRATED LIME ZEST

1. Prepare the grill.

2. In a small saucepan, melt the butter over medium heat until the foam disappears. Add the garlic, lime juice, and salt and cook, stirring occasionally with a wooden spoon, for 1 to 2 minutes, or until heated through. Remove the pan from the heat and stir in 2 tablespoons of the minced cilantro.

3. On each of four 12-inch metal skewers, thread 1 lime wedge followed by 3 chunks of monkfish, another lime wedge, 3 more chunks of monkfish, and finish with a lime wedge. Using a pastry brush, coat each of the skewers generously with some of the cilantro-lime butter.

4. Grill the skewers 4 inches from the heat, turning them, for 8 to 10 minutes, or until the fish is golden brown and the flesh flakes easily when tested with the tip of a knife.

5. Transfer the skewers to a heated platter, and drizzle them with the remaining butter. Combine the grated lime zest with an equal amount of the remaining minced cilantro and sprinkle it lightly over the hot skewers. Serve at once.

Salmon with Lemon Mayonnaise

SERVES 4

⏱ EXTRA-QUICK

1 TABLESPOON GRATED LEMON ZEST

2 TABLESPOONS FRESH LEMON JUICE

½ CUP MAYONNAISE

2 TABLESPOONS CHOPPED PARSLEY

¼ TEASPOON SALT

¼ TEASPOON WHITE PEPPER

4 SALMON FILLETS (ABOUT 1½ POUNDS TOTAL)

1. Prepare the grill. Spray a grilling basket with nonstick cooking spray.

2. In a small bowl, combine the lemon zest, lemon juice, mayonnaise, parsley, salt, and white pepper.

3. Place the salmon fillets, skin-side down, on the prepared grilling basket. Spread them with half of the lemon mayonnaise and close the basket. Grill the fish, skin-side down, 4 inches from the heat for 4 minutes; turn them, and grill for about 4 minutes more, until the topping is golden and slightly puffed. Divide the salmon fillets among 4 heated dinner plates and serve the remaining lemon mayonnaise on the side.

Sweet Afterthought: *For an elegant summer dessert, try grilled-peach sundaes. Allowing 1 peach per serving, blanch the fruit in boiling water for 2 to 3 minutes to loosen the skin, then peel and pit. Toss the peach halves with lemon juice, then place them on a lightly oiled grill and cook, basting occasionally with melted butter, for about 10 minutes, or until browned and somewhat softened. Slice the peaches and spoon them, while still warm, over vanilla ice cream; sprinkle with chopped toasted almonds.*

Tarragon-Marinated Salmon with Roasted Potatoes

SERVES 8

2¼ POUNDS SALMON FILLET

3 TABLESPOONS CHOPPED FRESH
TARRAGON

1 TABLESPOON SALT

2 TABLESPOONS LIGHT BROWN SUGAR

1 TABLESPOON VODKA

1½ TEASPOONS CRUSHED BLACK
PEPPERCORNS

¾ POUND VERY SMALL NEW POTATOES

1 TEASPOON SAFFLOWER OIL

DRIED FENNEL TWIGS TO BURN ON THE
COALS (OPTIONAL)

FENNEL LEAVES, FOR GARNISH

1. Lay the salmon in a large shallow dish. In a small bowl, mix the tarragon, salt, sugar, vodka, and 1 teaspoon of the peppercorns. Using the back of a spoon, spread the tarragon marinade all over the flesh side of the salmon. Cover the salmon loosely with a damp cloth, and let it marinate in the refrigerator at least 12 hours, or up to 48 hours.

2. Prepare the grill. Spray the grill rack with nonstick cooking spray. Soak 6 wooden skewers in cold water for 10 minutes.

3. In a large saucepan, cook the new potatoes in boiling water to cover until just tender when tested with a fork, 10 to 15 minutes. Drain and return the potatoes to the saucepan. Add the oil and the remaining crushed peppercorns, and toss the potatoes until they are evenly coated. Thread the potatoes onto the skewers and set aside.

4. Wipe all the marinade off the salmon. Place it, flesh-side down, on the grill 4 to 5 inches from the heat and grill it for 1 minute. Turn the salmon and grill it for 6 to 9 minutes more, until it is almost cooked through but not quite opaque in the center.

5. After 3 minutes, place the skewered potatoes on the rack and heat them, turning, until browned. At the same time, throw the dried fennel twigs, if you are using them, onto the coals to produce aromatic smoke.

6. Transfer the grilled salmon to a large heated platter. Remove the potatoes from the skewers and arrange them around the fish; garnish with the fennel leaves.

SALMON BARBECUED WITH DILL, LEMON, AND ONION

SERVES 4

⏱ EXTRA-QUICK

ONE 2½-POUND SALMON FILLET

3 TABLESPOONS OLIVE OIL

1 MEDIUM ONION, THINLY SLICED

3 LEMONS, CUT INTO ¼-INCH-THICK
  SLICES

1 SMALL BUNCH OF FRESH DILL, OR
  2 TEASPOONS DRIED

¼ TEASPOON SALT

⅛ TEASPOON BLACK PEPPER

1. Prepare the grill. Spray a grill basket with nonstick cooking spray.

2. Coat the salmon fillet on both sides with the olive oil, rubbing it into the flesh. Arrange the salmon in the grill basket and top it with a single layer of onion slices and the slices of 1 lemon. If using dried dill scatter it over the onion and lemon. Close the basket.

3. Lay the fresh dill, if using, on the grill rack, then position the grill basket on top of it. Cover the grill with the hood and grill the salmon, with the vent open, for 20 to 30 minutes, or until a meat thermometer placed in the thickest portion of the salmon registers 115°.

4. Using 2 metal spatulas, transfer the salmon to a cutting board or platter, sprinkle with the salt and pepper, and garnish with the remaining lemon slices.

Variation: *Grilling fish over fennel twigs is a French tradition, but this technique also works with other herbs. Try dill, cilantro, or rosemary sprigs, for a change. Large strips of fresh citrus peel also add a lovely flavor to fish. You can place the herbs or zest on the grill, as directed here, or scatter them directly onto the hot coals.*

GROUPER AND ROASTED PEPPERS

SERVES 4

1¼ POUNDS GROUPER FILLETS, SKIN
   LEFT ON, CUT INTO 4 PIECES
1½ TABLESPOONS OLIVE OIL
2 LIMES—1 JUICED, 1 CUT INTO
   WEDGES
½ TEASPOON SALT

⅛ TEASPOON BLACK PEPPER
1 LARGE RED BELL PEPPER
1 LARGE ORANGE BELL PEPPER
1 LARGE GREEN BELL PEPPER
1 TABLESPOON CHOPPED FRESH
   TARRAGON

1. Prepare the grill. Spray a grill basket with nonstick cooking spray.

2. Put the grouper, skin-side down, in a shallow dish. In a small bowl, combine the oil, lime juice, salt, and black pepper. Brush the marinade on the exposed side of the grouper. Let the fish marinate, covered, for 30 minutes.

3. Meanwhile, grill the bell peppers about 4 to 5 inches from the heat, turning them frequently, until their skins blacken, about 10 to 15 minutes. Remove the peppers from the grill and transfer them to a brown paper bag. Close the bag tightly.

4. When the peppers are cool enough to handle, peel off their skins. Derib, seed, and slice the skinned peppers thinly and evenly. Divide the slices among 4 dinner plates. Sprinkle the fresh tarragon on top.

5. Place the grouper in the grill basket and grill it, skin-side down, for 10 to 15 minutes. Turn the fish and grill for 5 minutes more.

6. Top each serving of bell peppers with a piece of grouper and garnish with a lime wedge. Serve immediately.

RED SNAPPER WITH RED PEPPER-CREAM SAUCE

SERVES 4

EXTRA-QUICK   LOW-FAT

½ SMALL RED BELL PEPPER, QUARTERED

½ SMALL ONION

1 GARLIC CLOVE, PEELED

2 TABLESPOONS DISTILLED WHITE
    VINEGAR

3 TABLESPOONS CREAM CHEESE, AT
    ROOM TEMPERATURE

1 TABLESPOON TOMATO PASTE

1 TABLESPOON PLAIN LOW-FAT YOGURT

1 TEASPOON CHILI POWDER

¼ TEASPOON SALT

PINCH OF BLACK PEPPER

4 RED SNAPPER FILLETS (ABOUT
    1¼ POUNDS TOTAL)

2 TABLESPOONS CHOPPED CHIVES OR
    SCALLION GREENS

1. Prepare the grill. Spray the grill rack with nonstick cooking spray.

2. Meanwhile, in a small saucepan, combine the bell pepper, onion, and garlic with ¼ cup of water and the vinegar. Bring the mixture to a boil over medium-high heat, reduce the heat to medium-low, and cover. Simmer until the vegetables are tender, about 10 minutes.

3. In a food processor, blend the cream cheese, tomato paste, and yogurt.

4. Drain the vegetables, add them to the food processor, and process until smooth. Blend in the chili powder, salt, and pepper.

5. Grill the red snapper fillets 4 inches from the heat until lightly colored, firm to the touch, and the flesh just flakes when tested with a fork, 4 to 5 minutes. Transfer the fish to a heated platter and top each fillet with some of the pepper-cream sauce. Sprinkle with the chopped chives or scallion greens.

SEA BASS GRILLED WITH LIME-GINGER SAUCE

SERVES 4

⏱ EXTRA-QUICK

2 TEASPOONS GRATED LIME ZEST

2 TABLESPOONS FRESH LIME JUICE

3 QUARTER-SIZE SLICES FRESH GINGER

3 TABLESPOONS SOY SAUCE

1 TABLESPOON VEGETABLE OIL

2 GARLIC CLOVES, MINCED

¼ TEASPOON RED PEPPER FLAKES

¼ TEASPOON BLACK PEPPER

1¼ POUNDS SEA BASS FILLETS OR
OTHER FIRM-FLESHED WHITE FISH

1. Preheat the grill. Spray the grill rack with nonstick cooking spray.

2. In a small bowl, combine the lime zest, lime juice, ginger, soy sauce, oil, garlic, red pepper flakes, and black pepper.

3. Place the sea bass fillets, skin-side up, on the grill and drizzle them evenly with some of the lime-ginger sauce. Grill the fish 4 inches from the heat for about 5 minutes. Turn the fish, baste with some of the lime-ginger sauce, and grill it for 4 to 5 minutes, or until the flesh is opaque and just flakes when tested with a fork.

4. Transfer the fish to a heated platter and serve the remaining sauce on the side.

Substitution: *Some other possible stand-ins for the sea bass are red snapper, grouper, or rockfish (called tilefish in the eastern United States). Be sure to get fillets that are at least 1 inch thick.*

Sesame Seafood Kebabs

SERVES 4

1 TEASPOON GRATED LEMON ZEST

1 TABLESPOON FRESH LEMON JUICE

1 CUP DRY WHITE WINE

1 TABLESPOON VEGETABLE OIL

1 GARLIC CLOVE, CRUSHED

⅛ TEASPOON SALT

PINCH OF BLACK PEPPER

¾ POUND MONKFISH FILLETS

1 TEASPOON CORNSTARCH

1 TABLESPOON CHOPPED MIXED FRESH
HERBS, SUCH AS BASIL, PARSLEY,
AND CHIVES

1 TABLESPOON SESAME SEEDS, TOASTED

4 LARGE SHRIMP

8 LARGE SEA SCALLOPS

SHREDDED LETTUCE, FOR GARNISH

1. In a small bowl, combine the lemon zest and lemon juice with ½ cup of the wine, the oil, garlic, salt, and pepper. Pour half of the mixture into a small saucepan and set aside.

2. Cut the monkfish into 12 equal pieces and add to the wine mixture in the bowl. Turn the pieces over in the marinade to coat them thoroughly. Cover the bowl and place it in the refrigerator for 1 to 2 hours.

3. Prepare the grill.

4. Add the remaining ½ cup wine to the saucepan. Blend the cornstarch to a smooth paste with a little cold water. Stir the paste into the liquid in the pan and heat it slowly, stirring constantly, until it boils and thickens. Remove the pan from the heat and stir in the mixed herbs and the sesame seeds. Cover the

pan and set it over very low heat to keep the sauce hot while the kebabs grill.

5. Lightly oil four 10-inch metal skewers. Drain the monkfish and thread the pieces onto the skewers, alternating them with the shrimp and scallops.

6. Grill the kebabs 4 to 5 inches from the heat for 3 to 5 minutes, turn the kebabs gently, and grill for 3 to 5 minutes. The fish is done when it is firm to the touch and the shellfish is lightly golden.

7. Spread the shredded lettuce on a large platter and pour the sauce into a warmed pitcher. Arrange the kebabs on the lettuce and serve them immediately, accompanied by the sauce.

SCALLOP AND BACON KEBABS

SERVES 4

🕐 EXTRA-QUICK

2 TABLESPOONS FRESH LEMON JUICE

1 TEASPOON SALT

¼ TEASPOON BLACK PEPPER

1 POUND SEA SCALLOPS, HALVED OR
  QUARTERED IF LARGE

8 SLICES LEAN BACON

1 STICK UNSALTED BUTTER, MELTED

1 LEMON, CUT LENGTHWISE INTO
  QUARTERS

1. Prepare the grill.

2. Combine the lemon juice, salt, and pepper in a small bowl and mix well. Drop in the scallops and stir them to coat evenly.

3. Thread the scallops and bacon onto four 10-inch metal skewers, looping the bacon slices up and down to weave them over and under the scallops. Push the scallops compactly together. With a pastry brush, thoroughly coat the scallops with a few spoonfuls of the melted butter.

4. Grill the skewers 4 inches from the heat, turning them and basting the scallops frequently with the remaining melted butter, for about 4 to 5 minutes. The scallops are done when they are opaque and firm to the touch, and the bacon is brown but not charred.

5. Slide the scallops and bacon off the skewers onto a heated platter. Serve with the lemon quarters.

SWEET AFTERTHOUGHT: *While you are enjoying your meal, a delicious dessert can be cooking in the coals. Core baking apples and fill the centers with a spoonful each of raisins, brown sugar, and butter. Wrap the apples securely in foil and place them directly in the coals. Bake for about 30 minutes, or until tender.*

BARBECUED GARLIC SHRIMP

SERVES 4 TO 6

2 POUNDS LARGE SHRIMP

1 CUP OLIVE OIL

2 TABLESPOONS RED WINE VINEGAR

1 TABLESPOON TOMATO PASTE

1 TABLESPOON OREGANO

2 TABLESPOONS MINCED GARLIC

3 TABLESPOONS FINELY CHOPPED
 PARSLEY

1 TEASPOON SALT

PINCH OF BLACK PEPPER

LEMON WEDGES, FOR GARNISH

1. Shell each shrimp carefully by breaking off the shell just above the point where it joins the tail, but don't remove the tail. With a small knife, make a shallow incision down the back of the shrimp and lift out the intestinal vein. Wash the shrimp thoroughly in cold water and pat them dry with paper towels.

2. In a large bowl, combine the oil, vinegar, tomato paste, oregano, garlic, parsley, salt, and pepper. Drop in the shrimp and stir gently to coat each well with the marinade. Cover and refrigerate for about 2 hours, stirring gently every ½ hour.

3. Prepare the grill.

4. Reserving the marinade, arrange the shrimp in 1 layer in a large grilling basket; close the basket. Grill the shrimp 4 to 5 inches from the heat for 3 minutes, then baste with the marinade. Grill for 2 minutes. Turn the shrimp, baste them with the marinade, and grill for 3 minutes, or until the shrimp are cooked through, but still moist, lightly colored, and firm to the touch. Be careful not to overcook.

5. Serve the barbecued shrimp on a large heated platter, garnished with the lemon wedges and with the remaining marinade, heated, on the side.

SHRIMP IN THE SHELL WITH HERBED MUSTARD BUTTER

SERVES 4

🕐 EXTRA-QUICK

1 STICK UNSALTED BUTTER, CUT INTO PIECES

2 GARLIC CLOVES, MINCED

½ CUP BEER

2 TABLESPOONS GRAINY MUSTARD

1½ TO 2 POUNDS LARGE UNSHELLED SHRIMP

¼ CUP CHOPPED FRESH ROSEMARY OR 1 TABLESPOON DRIED

1 TEASPOON CRUSHED BLACK PEPPERCORNS

1 BAY LEAF

¼ TEASPOON SALT

PARSLEY SPRIGS, FOR GARNISH

1. Prepare the grill. Spray a grill basket with nonstick cooking spray.

2. In a small saucepan, warm the butter with the garlic over low heat, being careful that the garlic does not brown.

3. In a glass bowl, whisk together the beer and mustard. Whisking constantly, drizzle in the garlic butter until thoroughly incorporated. Add the shrimp, rosemary, peppercorns, bay leaf, and salt, and, with a wooden spoon, stir to coat the shrimp.

4. Remove the shrimp from the sauce and arrange them in one layer in the grill basket; close the basket. Keep the sauce warm.

5. Grill the shrimp about 4 inches from the heat until they turn orange, 2 to 3 minutes per side. Return the grilled shrimp to the bowl, and toss to coat them with the reserved sauce. Serve immediately, garnished with the parsley sprigs.

CLAMBAKE ON THE GRILL

SERVES 4

12 HARD-SHELLED CLAMS

12 OYSTERS

2 MEDIUM LOBSTERS

1 CUP DRY WHITE WINE

1 TABLESPOON MINCED SHALLOT OR
ONION

PINCH OF SAFFRON THREADS

2 STICKS UNSALTED BUTTER, CUT INTO
PIECES

¼ TEASPOON SALT

⅛ TEASPOON BLACK PEPPER

6 FRESH BASIL LEAVES, CHOPPED, OR
½ TEASPOON DRIED

1. With a wire brush, scrub the clams and oysters thoroughly, and rinse in several changes of cold water.

2. Prepare the grill and when the fire is ready, add mesquite chips to flavor the smoke.

3. Set a sieve over a small saucepan. Using an oyster knife, open each oyster over the sieve, and pour the liquor through the sieve into the pan. Set aside. Loosen each oyster from its bottom shell and discard the bottom shell. Arrange the oysters in their half shells and the clams in a grilling basket; close the basket.

4. To kill the lobsters, plunge the tip of a knife into the lobster at the point where the body section and tail section meet. Make a small crosswise cut to sever the spinal cord.

5. Place the grilling basket on the grill about 4 to 5 inches from the heat and grill the clams and oysters for 10 to 12 minutes, or until the edges of the oysters are curled and the clams have opened. Remove the grilling basket from the grill. Add the lobsters to the grill and grill them for 5 to 7 minutes; turn and grill another 4 to 7 minutes, or until the shells have turned bright red.

6. Meanwhile, bring the oyster liquor to a boil over high heat. Add the wine and shallot, and reduce, stirring occasionally, to about 3 tablespoons, about 15 minutes. Crush the saffron threads and add to the sauce. Reduce the heat to low and start adding the butter to the sauce, 1 tablespoon at a time, whisking until thoroughly incorporated before adding the next. Add the salt and pepper. Remove the pan from the heat and stir in the basil. Divide the saffron butter among heated ramekins.

7. Transfer the lobsters, oysters, and clams to a heated platter and serve the saffron butter on the side.

SIDE DISHES

ROASTED HERBED POTATO FANS

SERVES 4

4 MEDIUM IDAHO POTATOES
4 TABLESPOONS UNSALTED BUTTER, AT
   ROOM TEMPERATURE
¼ TEASPOON PAPRIKA

¼ TEASPOON OREGANO
¼ TEASPOON BASIL
¼ TEASPOON SALT
PINCH OF BLACK PEPPER

1. Prepare the grill. Cut four 8-inch-square pieces of foil.

2. Cut the potatoes crosswise into ¼-inch-thick slices without cutting all the way through the flesh. Place each potato in the center of a square of foil, fold the edges together, and crimp to seal airtight.

3. Place the packets directly in the hot coals and cook, turning them several times, for about 40 minutes.

4. Meanwhile, cream the butter, then beat in the paprika, oregano, basil, salt, and pepper until blended and smooth.

5. With tongs, transfer the packets to a heated platter. Unwrap each, and with a pastry brush, spread each potato with some of the herbed butter, coating the inside surfaces of each slice. Rewrap the packets loosely and return the potatoes to the coals. Cook for 10 to 15 minutes more, or until the flesh yields easily when tested with the tines of a fork.

6. To serve, unwrap the packets, spread into fans, and serve at once.

VARIATION: *The luscious herbed butter can be used for many other grilled foods. Try it in foil-wrapped summer squash packets, over grilled onion halves, or as a super-indulgent topping for steaks.*

VEGETABLE PACKETS ON THE GRILL

SERVES 4

⏱ EXTRA-QUICK   ♡ LOW-FAT

8 SMALL LEEKS

4 MEDIUM ZUCCHINI, ENDS REMOVED

8 MEDIUM TOMATOES

¼ CUP CHOPPED FRESH BASIL, OR 2
    TABLESPOONS DRIED

½ CUP SWEET APPLE CIDER

¼ TEASPOON SALT

⅛ TEASPOON BLACK PEPPER

1. Prepare the grill. Cut four 12-inch squares of foil.

2. With a sharp knife, trim off and discard the tough green tops and roots from the leeks. Split the leeks lengthwise and rinse thoroughly under cold running water to remove all sand and grit. Quarter each zucchini lengthwise.

3. In a large saucepan of boiling water, blanch the tomatoes for 30 seconds. Transfer them to a colander and refresh under cold running water. Peel and seed the tomatoes, then quarter them.

4. Divide the chopped vegetables evenly among the foil squares and sprinkle each portion with basil and 2 tablespoons of the cider. Fold the edges of the foil together and crimp to seal airtight.

5. Place the packets on the grill and cook for 15 minutes. Before serving, unwrap the packets and season the vegetables with the salt and pepper.

GRILLED YELLOW AND GREEN BELL PEPPERS

SERVES 4

⏱ EXTRA-QUICK

2 YELLOW BELL PEPPERS

2 GREEN BELL PEPPERS

¼ CUP OLIVE OIL

6 GARLIC CLOVES, MINCED

¼ TEASPOON SALT

⅛ TEASPOON BLACK PEPPER

1. Prepare the grill.

2. Arrange the bell peppers around the edge of the grill, 4 inches from the heat. Grill, turning them often with tongs to make sure they char evenly, for 20 to 30 minutes, or until blackened all over. The yellow peppers will take about 5 minutes longer to grill than the green peppers.

3. Transfer the peppers to a paper bag, and close it tightly. Let the peppers steam in the bag until cool enough to handle, about 10 minutes. Peel the charred skin from the peppers, then core, quarter, and seed them.

4. In a small bowl, mix the oil and garlic.

5. Arrange the quartered peppers on a platter, alternating yellow and green pieces. Spoon the garlic oil over them, and season with the salt and pepper, or to taste.

KITCHEN NOTE: *Fire-roasted bell peppers are so delectable that it's a good idea to double or triple this recipe. Bell peppers are at their best—and their cheapest—in the summer, so why not roast a dozen or so? You can add the garlic oil or leave them plain. Place the peppers in small containers and store them in the refrigerator; they'll keep for about a week. Try sliced roasted peppers in turkey sandwiches, slivered peppers in salads, chopped peppers in omelets.*

ROASTED HERBED CORN ON THE COB

SERVES 4

🕐 EXTRA - QUICK

4 EARS OF CORN, UNHUSKED

4 TABLESPOONS UNSALTED BUTTER, AT
   ROOM TEMPERATURE

1 TEASPOON CHOPPED FRESH BASIL, OR
   ½ TEASPOON DRIED

1 TEASPOON CHOPPED FRESH
   OREGANO, OR ½ TEASPOON DRIED

¼ TEASPOON SALT

¼ TEASPOON BLACK PEPPER

1. Prepare the grill. Cut 4 large squares of foil for wrapping the corn.

2. Peel back but do not remove the corn husks on each ear. Remove and discard the corn silk.

3. In a small bowl, blend together the butter, basil, oregano, salt, and pepper.

4. Dividing evenly, spread the herbed butter over each ear of corn, then close the husk around the corn.

5. Wrap each ear of corn tightly in a square of foil. Place the wrapped ears in the coals and roast them, turning them occasionally, for 30 minutes, or until tender. Serve at once.

GRILLED VEGETABLE KEBABS

SERVES 8

 EXTRA-QUICK

½ CUP OLIVE OIL

2 GARLIC CLOVES, MINCED

2 TEASPOONS CHOPPED FRESH
    OREGANO, OR 1 TEASPOON DRIED

2 TEASPOONS CHOPPED FRESH BASIL,
    OR 1 TEASPOON DRIED

1 TEASPOON SALT

½ TEASPOON BLACK PEPPER

2 MEDIUM YELLOW SQUASH, CUT INTO
    1-INCH PIECES

2 MEDIUM GREEN BELL PEPPERS, CUT
    INTO 1-INCH SQUARES

16 CHERRY TOMATOES

16 MEDIUM MUSHROOMS

1. Prepare the grill.

2. In a small bowl, stir together the oil, garlic, oregano, basil, salt, and pepper.

3. Alternating the vegetables, thread them onto eight 10-inch metal skewers, beginning and ending each skewer with a mushroom.

Brush the skewered vegetables with the olive oil mixture.

4. Grill the kebabs 4 inches from the heat, turning and basting them frequently, for about 5 minutes per side, or until the vegetables are tender.

SUBSTITUTION: *Miniature summer squashes—of a size suitable for a doll's dinner table—make a pretty replacement for the cut-up yellow squash. You can use tiny zucchini or yellow squash.*

ROASTED RED PEPPER, SNOW PEA, AND TOMATO SALAD

SERVES 4

🕐 EXTRA-QUICK

3 SMALL RED BELL PEPPERS

¼ POUND SNOW PEAS, STRINGS REMOVED, OR TINY GREEN BEANS

1 TABLESPOON DIJON MUSTARD

½ TEASPOON CREOLE MUSTARD

2 SCALLIONS, FINELY CHOPPED

2 TABLESPOONS TARRAGON VINEGAR OR WHITE WINE VINEGAR

¼ CUP MINCED FRESH TARRAGON, OR 1 TEASPOON DRIED

½ CUP OLIVE OIL

¼ TEASPOON SALT

⅛ TEASPOON BLACK PEPPER

1 SMALL HEAD OF BOSTON LETTUCE, SEPARATED INTO LEAVES

2 MEDIUM TOMATOES, CUT INTO ½-INCH-THICK SLICES

1. Prepare the grill.

2. Place the bell peppers on the grill rack and roast them, turning them until the skins are blackened all over, about 10 minutes in all. With tongs, remove the charred peppers to a paper bag, close it tightly, and let the peppers steam until cool enough to handle, about 15 minutes.

3. In a small saucepan, blanch the snow peas or green beans in boiling water for 2 minutes. Drain in a colander and refresh under cold running water; pat dry with paper towels.

4. In a bowl, combine the mustards, scallions, vinegar, and tarragon, whisking until smooth. Gradually drizzle in the oil, whisking constantly, until the dressing is thick and smooth and the consistency of mayonnaise. Add the salt and pepper.

5. Remove the peppers from the bag and peel off the charred skins. Halve, seed, and derib the peppers. Cut into ½-inch-wide strips.

6. Line a platter with the lettuce leaves and arrange the tomatoes, snow peas, and roasted pepper strips decoratively on top. Pour the dressing over the salad.

HERBED NEW POTATOES, CARROTS, AND SCALLIONS

SERVES 4

16 SMALL NEW POTATOES

12 BABY CARROTS, PEELED

9 SCALLIONS, TRIMMED, LEAVING 2
INCHES OF GREEN, OR 18 PEARL
ONIONS, PEELED

½ CUP OLIVE OIL

1 TABLESPOON MINCED FRESH SAGE,
ROSEMARY, OR THYME, OR 1
TEASPOON DRIED

¼ TEASPOON SALT

⅛ TEASPOON BLACK PEPPER

1. Prepare the grill.

2. In a large bowl, combine the potatoes, carrots, and scallions or onions, and drizzle the olive oil over all; toss until evenly coated. Sprinkle the vegetables with sage, rosemary, or thyme and toss again.

3. Cut four 12-inch squares of foil and divide the potatoes and carrots evenly among them. Transfer the potatoes and carrots to the lower half of each piece of foil and arrange them in a single layer. Fold down the top half of square, being careful not to disturb the vegetables, and crimp the edges to seal. Reserve the oil remaining in the bowl.

4. Place the packets on the grill and cook for 15 minutes.

5. With tongs or a metal spatula, carefully remove the packets from the grill. Open the packets and add the scallions or onions next to, not on top of, the potatoes and carrots. Drizzle the remaining herbed oil over them. Reseal the packets and place on grill, turning them so that the "uncooked" side is down. Grill for 15 minutes. Remove the packets from the grill and leave sealed until ready to serve.

6. To serve, open the packets and turn the vegetables into a heated serving bowl; season with the salt and pepper, or to taste.

Macaroni and Bell Pepper Salad

S E R V E S   4

2 CUPS ELBOW MACARONI

1 TEASPOON VEGETABLE OIL

1 CUP MAYONNAISE

¼ CUP CIDER VINEGAR

3 TABLESPOONS DIJON MUSTARD

⅓ CUP CHOPPED CILANTRO

1½ TEASPOONS CELERY SEEDS, CRUSHED

½ TEASPOON SALT

½ TEASPOON BLACK PEPPER

⅛ TEASPOON CAYENNE PEPPER

1 CUP DICED GREEN BELL PEPPER

1 CUP DICED CARROTS

1 CUP CHOPPED PITTED BLACK OLIVES

1. In a large saucepan of boiling salted water, cook the macaroni according to package directions, until tender but still firm. Drain, rinse under cold running water, and drain again. Return the macaroni to the pan and toss it with the oil; set aside.

2. In a large bowl, combine the mayonnaise, vinegar, mustard, cilantro, celery seeds, salt, black pepper, and cayenne pepper, and stir until well blended.

3. Add the macaroni, bell pepper, carrots, and olives to the dressing, and toss gently until the macaroni is well coated. Cover the bowl and refrigerate the salad for at least 1 hour, or until the flavors are blended.

Variation: *For a slightly more sophisticated salad, use grilled peppers (see page 86) instead of the fresh green bell pepper. And for the pasta, try radiatore, a "fancier" substitute for good old elbow macaroni.*

SHREDDED CARROT SALAD WITH PECANS AND RED ONION

SERVES 6

6 MEDIUM CARROTS, PEELED

1 SMALL RED ONION

¾ CUP MAYONNAISE

4 TABLESPOONS FRESH LEMON JUICE

2 TEASPOONS GRATED LEMON ZEST

1 TABLESPOON DIJON MUSTARD

1 TEASPOON DRY MUSTARD

¼ TEASPOON BLACK PEPPER

¼ TEASPOON SUGAR

1 CUP CHOPPED PECANS

1 CUP GOLDEN RAISINS

1. In a food processor, shred the carrots.

2. Halve the onion lengthwise, then cut it crosswise into thin half-rings.

3. In a large serving bowl, combine the mayonnaise, lemon juice, lemon zest, Dijon and dry mustards, pepper, and sugar.

4. Add the carrots, onion, pecans, and raisins, and toss to combine. Refrigerate for at least 1 hour before serving.

SUBSTITUTION: *For a salad that's lower in fat, stir together ¼ cup plain low-fat yogurt (or fat-free sour cream) and ¼ cup low-fat mayonnaise; substitute this mixture for the mayonnaise. Reducing the amount of pecans will also cut calories and fat.*

RATATOUILLE WITH MUSHROOMS

SERVES 8

1½ POUNDS EGGPLANT, PEELED AND
    CUT INTO 1-INCH PIECES
1½ TEASPOONS SALT
2 TABLESPOONS OLIVE OIL
2 LARGE ONIONS, CUT INTO THIN
    RINGS
4 GARLIC CLOVES, CRUSHED
¼ CUP DRY WHITE WINE
½ POUND LARGE MUSHROOMS,
    STEMMED AND SLICED

3 TABLESPOONS CHOPPED FRESH
    OREGANO, OR 1 TABLESPOON DRIED
2 YELLOW BELL PEPPERS, BLANCHED
    AND CUT INTO 2½-INCH-LONG
    STRIPS
1 POUND PLUM TOMATOES, PEELED,
    SEEDED, AND COARSELY CHOPPED
    INTO ½-INCH PIECES
⅛ TEASPOON BLACK PEPPER
3 TABLESPOONS CHOPPED FRESH BASIL

1. In a medium bowl, toss the eggplant pieces with 1 teaspoon of the salt. Place eggplant in a colander and weight it down with a plate small enough to rest on top of the pieces. Let the eggplant stand for 30 minutes.

2. Rinse the eggplant under cold running water and drain it well. Pat the pieces dry on paper towels.

3. In a large saucepan, warm the oil. Add the onions and cook them over low heat, stirring occasionally, until soft but not brown, about 8 minutes. Add the garlic and cook, stirring for 1 minute.

4. Add the eggplant pieces, pour in the wine, and cook, uncovered, stirring, for 15 minutes. Stir in the mushrooms and oregano, cover the pan, and cook the mixture for 5 minutes.

5. Add the yellow peppers, the tomatoes, the remaining ½ teaspoon salt, and the black pepper. Cook, stirring, until heated through, about 5 minutes. Remove the pan from the heat and stir in the basil. Transfer the ratatouille to a wide, shallow serving bowl and let it cool to room temperature.

Hot German Potato Salad

SERVES 6 TO 8

12 MEDIUM RED POTATOES
6 SLICES BACON (ABOUT ¼ POUND
   TOTAL)
1 MEDIUM RED ONION, CHOPPED
3 TABLESPOONS FLOUR
1½ TABLESPOONS SUGAR
¾ TEASPOON DRY MUSTARD
¾ TEASPOON SALT
½ TEASPOON CELERY SEEDS

½ TEASPOON BLACK PEPPER
⅔ CUP CIDER VINEGAR
3 HARD-COOKED EGGS, COARSELY
   CHOPPED
1 SMALL GREEN BELL PEPPER, CHOPPED
1 CUP CHOPPED CELERY, INCLUDING
   THE LEAVES
¼ CUP CHOPPED PARSLEY

1. In a large saucepan of simmering salted water, cook the potatoes until tender, 30 to 35 minutes. Drain and set aside.

2. Meanwhile, in a large skillet, cook the bacon over medium heat until crisp, about 10 minutes. Reserving the fat, remove the bacon; crumble and set aside.

3. In the bacon fat, sauté the onion over medium heat until softened but not brown, about 10 minutes. Stir in the flour, sugar, mustard, salt, celery seeds, and black pepper. Reduce the heat to low and cook, stirring constantly, until the mixture has slightly thickened, about 5 minutes.

4. Remove the skillet from the heat and stir in ¾ cup of water and the vinegar. Return the skillet to the heat and bring to a boil, stirring constantly. Cook, stirring, for 1 minute. Remove the skillet from the heat and stir in the reserved crumbled bacon.

5. Slice the unpeeled potatoes into the dressing and stir gently to coat. Return the skillet to medium heat and cook, stirring gently, until the dressing is hot and bubbly, about 1 minute.

6. Transfer the hot potato salad to a large serving bowl. Stir in the eggs, green pepper, celery, and parsley. Serve the salad warm.

BROCCOLI SALAD WITH RED ONION AND YELLOW PEPPER

SERVES 6

 EXTRA-QUICK

4 CUPS CHOPPED BROCCOLI

2 GARLIC CLOVES, UNPEELED

¼ CUP OLIVE OIL

2 TABLESPOONS RED WINE VINEGAR

1½ TEASPOONS DRY MUSTARD

½ TEASPOON SALT

¼ TEASPOON BLACK PEPPER

3 TABLESPOONS CHOPPED CHIVES OR SCALLION GREENS

1 LARGE YELLOW BELL PEPPER, CUT INTO THIN STRIPS

1 SMALL RED ONION, CUT INTO THIN SLICES

1. Steam the broccoli and the garlic in a steamer until the broccoli is tender, 5 to 8 minutes.

2. Remove the garlic cloves from the steamer and set aside. Cool the broccoli by refreshing it under cold running water; drain well.

3. In a small bowl, whisk together the oil, vinegar, mustard, salt, pepper, and chives.

Peel the cooked garlic and mash it with a fork; add it to the dressing, whisking well to blend.

4. Place the broccoli, bell pepper, onion, and dressing in a salad bowl and toss to combine.

VARIATION: *Make the salad with half broccoli and half cauliflower, or all cauliflower, or try it with broccoflower, a newly introduced vegetable that's a cross between the two.*

Pasta Salad with Pesto

SERVES 4 TO 6

🕐 EXTRA-QUICK

1 POUND PASTA SHELLS

½ CUP GRATED ROMANO OR PARMESAN CHEESE

2 CUPS FRESH BASIL LEAVES

2 GARLIC CLOVES, COARSELY CHOPPED

½ CUP PECAN HALVES

½ CUP OLIVE OIL

½ TEASPOON SALT

¼ TEASPOON BLACK PEPPER

1. In a large saucepan, bring 2 quarts salted water to a boil. Add the pasta and cook, stirring occasionally, according to the package directions. Drain. Transfer to a large serving bowl.

2. Meanwhile, in a food processor, combine the cheese, basil leaves, garlic, and pecans and pulse until puréed. With the machine running, through the feed tube, slowly pour in the olive oil; process until combined. Season the pesto with the salt and pepper or to taste.

3. Pour the pesto over the warm shells and toss gently to combine. Cool to room temperature before serving.

Kitchen Note: *Resist the temptation to use pre-grated cheese in this recipe. The brand-name grated Parmesan and Romano sold in containers is vastly inferior to cheese you grate yourself—assuming that you have a good-quality cheese to begin with. If possible, get a well-aged Parmesan or Romano imported from Italy.*

CORN AND RED PEPPER SALAD

SERVES 4

EXTRA-QUICK

¼ CUP OLIVE OIL

6 LARGE SHALLOTS, CHOPPED

2 MEDIUM RED BELL PEPPERS, CUT
   INTO STRIPS

¼ TEASPOON SALT

⅛ TEASPOON BLACK PEPPER

4 EARS FRESH CORN OR TWO
   10-OUNCE PACKAGES FROZEN
   CORN KERNELS, THAWED

1 GARLIC CLOVE, MINCED

½ TEASPOON BLACK PEPPERCORNS,
   CRUSHED

1 TEASPOON CHOPPED FRESH THYME,
   OR 1 TEASPOON DRIED

1½ TEASPOONS CHOPPED PARSLEY

3 TABLESPOONS DRY WHITE WINE

2 TEASPOONS SHERRY VINEGAR OR RED
   WINE VINEGAR

1. In a large skillet, warm 2 tablespoons of the oil over medium heat for 30 seconds. Reduce the heat to low, add the shallots, and cook, stirring frequently, until translucent and crisp-tender, 4 to 5 minutes. Transfer the shallots to a large serving bowl.

2. Add the remaining 2 tablespoons oil to the pan and warm over medium-low heat. Add the red peppers and cook over medium-low heat, stirring frequently, until just barely tender, about 10 minutes. Season the peppers with the salt and pepper and transfer them to the bowl with the shallots.

3. If using fresh corn, cut the kernels from the ears. Add the corn (fresh or frozen) to the skillet and cook, stirring frequently, until heated through, about 6 minutes for fresh, 3 minutes for frozen.

4. Add the garlic and crushed black peppercorns and stir to combine. Transfer the corn to the bowl with the shallots and peppers.

5. Add the thyme, parsley, white wine, and vinegar and stir to combine. Let the salad cool to room temperature, stirring occasionally.

GREEK GREEN BEAN SALAD

SERVES 4

⏱ EXTRA-QUICK

1 POUND FRESH GREEN BEANS, CUT
INTO 2-INCH PIECES

3 TABLESPOONS OLIVE OIL

3 TABLESPOONS RED WINE VINEGAR OR
CIDER VINEGAR

1 GARLIC CLOVE, MINCED

2 TEASPOONS CHOPPED FRESH
OREGANO, OR 1 TEASPOON DRIED

¼ TEASPOON BLACK PEPPER

1 SMALL RED ONION, THINLY SLICED

½ CUP OIL-CURED PITTED BLACK
OLIVES, COARSELY CHOPPED

½ CUP CRUMBLED FETA CHEESE

1. Place the green beans in a vegetable steamer and bring the water to a boil. Steam the beans until crisp-tender, about 8 minutes. Cool the beans in a colander under cold running water.

2. Meanwhile, in a small bowl, combine the oil, vinegar, garlic, oregano, and pepper.

3. In a salad bowl, combine the green beans, onion, olives, and dressing, and toss to coat well. Top the salad with the crumbled feta.

4. Serve the salad at room temperature or cover and chill until ready to serve.

HONEY-MUSTARD COLESLAW

SERVES 4

⏱ EXTRA-QUICK

½ POUND GREEN CABBAGE, TOUGH
   OUTER LEAVES REMOVED

½ POUND RED CABBAGE, CORED AND
   TOUGH OUTER LEAVES REMOVED

1 SMALL ZUCCHINI

1 SMALL CARROT

1 SHALLOT, MINCED

12 SMALL SWEET PICKLES, EACH
   SLICED ¼ TO ½ INCH THICK

2 TABLESPOONS FRESH LEMON JUICE

1 TABLESPOON WHITE WINE VINEGAR

1 TABLESPOON CHOPPED FRESH DILL

1 TABLESPOON CHOPPED PARSLEY

¼ CUP PREPARED HONEY MUSTARD, OR
   EQUAL PARTS DIJON MUSTARD AND
   HONEY

⅓ CUP MAYONNAISE

¼ TEASPOON SALT

⅛ TEASPOON BLACK PEPPER

1. In a food processor or on the large holes of a box grater, finely shred the cabbages. Transfer the cabbage to a large bowl and toss to combine the colors.

2. In the food processor or on the large holes of the grater, shred the zucchini and carrot. Add the zucchini, carrot, shallot, pickles, lemon juice, vinegar, dill, and parsley to the bowl and toss to combine.

3. In a small bowl, blend the honey mustard and mayonnaise. Spoon the mixture over the slaw and toss until blended. Add the salt and pepper and toss again. Cover and chill thoroughly before serving.

VARIATION: *You can use 1 tablespoon of the liquid from the pickle jar in place of the vinegar. And if the sweet slant of this slaw does not appeal to you, use kosher dill pickles instead of sweet pickles. In addition, make the dressing with just ¼ cup Dijon mustard rather than the honey-mustard blend.*

Tomato, Onion, and Arugula Salad

SERVES 4

EXTRA-QUICK

1 TEASPOON SESAME SEEDS

2 BUNCHES OF ARUGULA, STEMMED, OR 1 HEAD OF BOSTON LETTUCE

1 POUND TOMATOES, COARSELY CHOPPED

1 SMALL RED ONION, CUT INTO THIN SLICES

1 MEDIUM ORANGE, PEELED AND SEPARATED INTO SECTIONS

2 TABLESPOONS RED WINE VINEGAR

1 TEASPOON TAMARI, OR ½ TEASPOON SOY SAUCE

1 TABLESPOON FRESH LEMON JUICE

⅛ TEASPOON SALT

PINCH OF BLACK PEPPER

¼ CUP VEGETABLE OIL

1. In a small skillet, toast the sesame seeds over medium heat until they turn golden brown and release their fragrance, about 3 to 4 minutes.

2. In a salad bowl, combine the arugula, tomatoes, onion, and orange sections, and toss to combine.

3. In a small bowl, combine the vinegar, tamari or soy sauce, lemon juice, salt, and pepper and whisk in the oil until the dressing is combined.

4. Pour the dressing over the salad, toss gently, and sprinkle the sesame seeds on top.

Shaker Green Bean Salad

SERVES 4

⏱ EXTRA-QUICK

½ POUND FRESH GREEN BEANS, CUT
   INTO 2-INCH PIECES
¼ CUP TARRAGON VINEGAR
1 TEASPOON DIJON MUSTARD
1 TEASPOON CHOPPED FRESH
   TARRAGON, OR ½ TEASPOON DRIED
½ TEASPOON SALT
¼ TEASPOON BLACK PEPPER

1 TABLESPOON CAPERS (OPTIONAL)
2 MEDIUM SHALLOTS, MINCED, OR 2
   TABLESPOONS MINCED ONION
1 CUP CHOPPED SCALLIONS
½ CUP OLIVE OIL
1 HEAD OF BIBB OR BOSTON LETTUCE,
   TORN INTO BITE-SIZE PIECES

1. In a large saucepan of simmering salted water, cook the beans until crisp-tender, 2 to 3 minutes. Drain, rinse under cold running water, and drain again. Cover the beans and refrigerate until ready to serve.

2. Just before serving, in a salad bowl, combine the vinegar, mustard, tarragon, salt, pepper, capers (if using), shallots, and scallions. Gradually whisk in the olive oil.

3. Add the green beans and lettuce, toss the salad gently, and serve.

Substitution: *The tarragon vinegar adds an extra herbal touch to the salad, but if you're unable to find it at your market, you can use cider vinegar or white wine vinegar in its place. Conversely, you can further reinforce the herb flavor by using tarragon mustard, which is sold in gourmet shops and some supermarkets.*

POTATO CAKES WITH
SCALLION SOUR CREAM

EXTRA-QUICK

½ CUP SOUR CREAM

½ CUP FINELY CHOPPED SCALLIONS

¾ TEASPOON BLACK PEPPER

2 POUNDS ALL-PURPOSE POTATOES

2 EGGS, LIGHTLY BEATEN

¼ CUP FLOUR

2 GARLIC CLOVES, MINCED

¼ TEASPOON SALT

2 TABLESPOONS OLIVE OIL

1. In a small bowl, combine the sour cream, scallions, and ½ teaspoon of the pepper, and stir until blended. Cover and refrigerate until needed.

2. Peel the potatoes, then grate them on the coarse side of a grater into a large bowl. Add the eggs, flour, garlic, salt, and the remaining pepper, and stir until well blended.

3. Warm 1 teaspoon of the oil in a large skillet over medium heat. Drop ¼-cup portions of the potato mixture into the skillet and flatten each portion into a cake. Cook the potato cakes until the edges are crisp and browned, 3 to 4 minutes, then turn them and cook until golden brown, 3 to 4 minutes. Transfer the cooked potato cakes to a warm platter and cover them with foil to keep warm. Cook the remaining potato mixture in the same way, adding more oil, as needed.

4. Serve the potato cakes with the scallion sour cream.

Oven-Fried Potato Wedges

SERVES 8

8 MEDIUM BAKING POTATOES

4 TABLESPOONS UNSALTED BUTTER,
  MELTED

¼ CUP OLIVE OIL

2 GARLIC CLOVES, MINCED

¾ TEASPOON SALT

¼ TEASPOON BLACK PEPPER

½ CUP GRATED ROMANO CHEESE

1. Preheat the oven to 400°. Line a baking sheet with foil.

2. Cut each potato lengthwise into 8 wedges.

3. Stir together the butter, olive oil, garlic, salt, and pepper.

4. Place the potato wedges on the prepared baking sheet and brush them with the butter mixture. Sprinkle them with the cheese and bake, turning occasionally, for 40 minutes, or until the potatoes are browned.

VARIATION: *While many people think of brown sugar and marshmallows as the appropriate additions to sweet potatoes, savory seasonings also combine well with these highly nutritious root vegetables. Try substituting them for the baking potatoes in this recipe, but note that the baking time may be shorter: You'll want to check for doneness after about 30 minutes.*

COWBOY BEANS

SERVES 8

♡ LOW-FAT

ONE 14-OUNCE CAN NO-SALT-ADDED
   WHOLE TOMATOES

1 TABLESPOON CHOPPED MILD GREEN
   CHILIES

½ CUP FINELY CHOPPED GREEN BELL
   PEPPER

½ CUP MINCED ONION

1 SMALL JALAPEÑO PEPPER, SEEDED
   AND MINCED

3 TABLESPOONS TOMATO PASTE

2 TABLESPOONS DIJON MUSTARD

1½ TABLESPOONS BROWN SUGAR

½ TEASPOON DRY MUSTARD

½ TEASPOON SALT

⅛ TEASPOON BLACK PEPPER

1 BAY LEAF

TWO 19-OUNCE CANS PINTO BEANS,
   RINSED AND DRAINED

1. Preheat the oven to 350°.

2. In a large pot, combine 1 cup of water with the tomatoes, chilies, bell pepper, onion, jalapeño pepper, tomato paste, Dijon mustard, sugar, dry mustard, salt, black pepper, and the bay leaf. Bring the mixture to a boil over medium-high heat, stirring and breaking up the tomatoes. Reduce the heat to low and simmer, stirring occasionally, for 30 minutes. Remove the bay leaf.

3. Transfer the contents of the pot to a large casserole. Add the beans and stir to combine. Cover and bake for 45 minutes.

CORN PUDDING

SERVES 4 TO 6

3 EGGS
1 CUP HEAVY CREAM
1 CUP MILK
2 TABLESPOONS FLOUR
2 TEASPOONS SUGAR
¼ TEASPOON NUTMEG

¼ TEASPOON SALT
⅛ TEASPOON CAYENNE PEPPER
3 CUPS FROZEN CORN KERNELS,
   THAWED
1½ CUPS CHOPPED SCALLIONS

1. Preheat the oven to 375°. Butter a shallow 1½-quart baking dish.

2. In a large bowl, blend the eggs, cream, and milk. Add the flour, sugar, nutmeg, salt, and cayenne pepper. Stir in the corn and scallions.

3. Turn the mixture into the prepared baking dish. Set the baking dish into a larger pan and place in the oven. Pour enough hot water into the larger pan to come halfway up the sides of the baking dish. Bake for 1 hour, or until a knife inserted in the center comes out clean.

KITCHEN NOTE: *You can cut the kernels from fresh corn with a knife, but there is also a simple tool for this job, available in many kitchen stores. It's a trough-shaped device somewhat longer than an ear of corn. Various blades are set around an opening in the center of the trough; they cut the kernels from the corn as you slide the cob back and forth.*

CUCUMBER-ONION SALAD

SERVES 4

2 MEDIUM CUCUMBERS
2 TEASPOONS SALT
⅓ CUP CIDER VINEGAR
⅓ CUP SOUR CREAM
3 TABLESPOONS LIGHT BROWN SUGAR

½ TEASPOON DIJON MUSTARD
¼ TEASPOON BLACK PEPPER
1 MEDIUM RED ONION, THINLY SLICED
2 TABLESPOONS CHOPPED PARSLEY, FOR
   GARNISH

1. With a vegetable peeler, remove lengthwise strips of cucumber peel to create a striped pattern on the cucumbers.

2. Cut the cucumbers into thin rounds and place in a colander. Sprinkle the cucumber slices with the salt, toss well, and let stand for 15 minutes. Rinse the cucumbers well and pat dry.

3. In a small bowl, whisk together the vinegar, sour cream, brown sugar, mustard, and pepper. Place the cucumbers and sliced onion in a serving bowl, pour the dressing over them, and toss to coat. Refrigerate for at least 2 hours, or until ready to serve.

4. Garnish the salad with the chopped parsley just before serving.

KITCHEN NOTE: *European (hothouse) cucumbers, or diminutive kirbies (also called pickling cucumbers), have thin, unwaxed skins that make them the best candidates for this salad. They also tend to be crisper than regular cucumbers.*

THREE-BEAN SALAD

SERVES 8 TO 10

¼ POUND FRESH GREEN BEANS, CUT INTO 2-INCH LENGTHS

2½ CUPS CANNED KIDNEY BEANS, RINSED AND DRAINED

3 CUPS CANNED CHICKPEAS, RINSED AND DRAINED

1 MEDIUM YELLOW BELL PEPPER, CUT INTO 1-INCH SQUARES

1 MEDIUM RED BELL PEPPER, CUT INTO 1-INCH SQUARES

1½ CUPS CHOPPED SCALLIONS

2 GARLIC CLOVES, MINCED

¼ CUP OLIVE OIL

¼ CUP RED WINE VINEGAR

2 TABLESPOONS FRESH LEMON JUICE

1 TABLESPOON DIJON MUSTARD

2 TEASPOONS SALT

½ TEASPOON BLACK PEPPER

½ TEASPOON SUGAR

1 HEAD OF BOSTON LETTUCE, SEPARATED INTO LEAVES

1. In a saucepan of simmering salted water, blanch the green beans until crisp-tender, about 1 minute. Rinse in cold water, drain, and set aside.

2. In a large serving bowl, combine the kidney beans, chickpeas, green beans, yellow pepper, red pepper, and scallions.

3. In a small bowl, blend the garlic, oil, vinegar, lemon juice, mustard, salt, black pepper, and sugar. Pour the dressing over the salad and toss well to combine.

4. Cover and refrigerate the salad for at least 2½ hours (or longer for more flavor), tossing occasionally to coat the vegetables evenly with the dressing.

5. To serve, line a serving platter with the Boston lettuce leaves and spoon the bean salad on top.

RED POTATO SALAD

SERVES 4

1 POUND RED POTATOES, UNPEELED

¼ CUP MAYONNAISE

2 TABLESPOONS OLIVE OIL

2 TABLESPOONS RED WINE VINEGAR

2 TABLESPOONS CAPERS, DRAINED
   (OPTIONAL)

½ TEASPOON THYME

¼ TEASPOON BLACK PEPPER

½ TEASPOON SALT

1 LARGE YELLOW OR RED BELL PEPPER,
   CUT INTO BITE-SIZE PIECES

1. Halve the potatoes if they are large. Steam them in a vegetable steamer until they are tender, about 15 minutes.

2. Meanwhile, in a medium bowl, combine the mayonnaise, oil, vinegar, capers (if using), thyme, pepper, and salt.

3. When the potatoes are done, add them, while they are still hot, to the dressing and toss to coat. Let cool to room temperature.

4. Add the peppers to the cooled potatoes and toss to combine. Cover with plastic wrap and refrigerate for at least 2 hours.

SUMMER FRUIT SALAD
WITH YOGURT DRESSING

SERVES 6

⏱ EXTRA-QUICK ♡ LOW-FAT

1 LARGE PINEAPPLE
1 CUP BLUEBERRIES
½ MEDIUM CANTALOUPE
1 PINT STRAWBERRIES

2 LIMES
1 CUP PLAIN LOW-FAT YOGURT
2 TABLESPOONS HONEY
½ TEASPOON VANILLA EXTRACT

1. Halve the pineapple lengthwise, leaving the leaves on and cutting through the crown. Using a grapefruit knife (or other sharp flexible knife), loosen the fruit from the skin of the pineapple, leaving a ½-inch-thick shell; set the pineapple shells aside. Cut the cores out of the pineapple flesh and cut the fruit into bite-size pieces. Place the pineapple pieces in a medium bowl with the blueberries.

2. With a melon baller or teaspoon, scoop the flesh out of the cantaloupe half. Add the cantaloupe balls or pieces to the bowl. Halve the strawberries and add half of them to the fruit in the bowl; set the remaining strawberries aside.

3. Grate the zest from the limes, then juice them. Add the lime juice and zest to the bowl of fruit and toss to combine.

4. Dividing evenly, scoop the fruit salad into the pineapple shells.

5. In a serving bowl, mash the remaining strawberries with a fork. Stir in the yogurt, honey, and vanilla and stir until combined.

6. Serve the pineapple halves on a platter, with the dressing on the side.

TROPICAL FRUIT SALAD WITH CANDIED GINGER

SERVES 6

⏱ EXTRA-QUICK ♡ LOW-FAT

4 VERY RIPE PASSIONFRUITS

½ HONEYDEW MELON, SCOOPED INTO BALLS WITH A MELON BALLER

½ CANTALOUPE, SCOOPED INTO BALLS WITH A MELON BALLER

½ PINEAPPLE, CORED AND CUT INTO CHUNKS

2 GUAVAS, HALVED LENGTHWISE, SEEDED, EACH HALF SLICED CROSSWISE

1 PINK GRAPEFRUIT, PEELED AND CUT INTO SEGMENTS

2 PAPAYAS, PEELED AND SEEDED, FLESH CUT INTO CHUNKS

1 LARGE MANGO, PEELED, FLESH CUT LENGTHWISE INTO SLICES

¼ CUP CANDIED GINGER, COARSELY CHOPPED

CHOPPED PECANS, FOR GARNISH (OPTIONAL)

1. Cut the passionfruits in half crosswise. Using a teaspoon, scoop out the seeds and pulp from each fruit into a fine sieve set over a bowl. With the back of a spoon, press all the juice into the bowl; discard the seeds and fibrous pulp remaining in the sieve.

2. Place all the prepared fruits in a large serving bowl and pour on the passionfruit juice.

Gently mix and turn the fruits in the bowl to coat with juice. Chill the fruit salad, covered with plastic wrap, in the refrigerator.

3. Just before serving, add the candied ginger and stir it gently but thoroughly into the fruit salad. Garnish with the chopped pecans, if desired, and serve the salad at once on slightly chilled plates.

MARINADES AND SAUCES

Lemon-Pepper Marinade

SERVES 6 TO 8

⏱ EXTRA-QUICK

⅓ CUP OLIVE OIL

1 TABLESPOON GRATED LEMON ZEST

¼ CUP PLUS 2 TABLESPOONS FRESH
   LEMON JUICE

1½ TEASPOONS SUGAR

1¼ TEASPOONS BLACK PEPPER

1 TEASPOON SALT

2 TABLESPOONS CHOPPED FRESH
   PARSLEY

1. In a small bowl, combine the oil, lemon zest, lemon juice, sugar, pepper, salt, and the parsley. Marinate fish for 30 minutes, chicken up to 2 hours. (If marinating for more than 1 hour, cover and refrigerate.)

Kitchen Note: *This recipe makes enough for 1 to 2 pounds of chicken cutlets or fish fillets. Spoon a little of the marinade over the meat a few minutes before it's done for an extra flavor kick.*

PESTO MARINADE

SERVES 6 TO 8

EXTRA-QUICK

1½ CUPS FRESH BASIL LEAVES

3 TABLESPOONS OLIVE OIL

2 TABLESPOONS GRATED PARMESAN
CHEESE

2 TABLESPOONS CHICKEN BROTH

2 TABLESPOONS FRESH LEMON JUICE

2 GARLIC CLOVES, PEELED

¼ TEASPOON BLACK PEPPER

⅛ TEASPOON SALT

1. In a food processor or blender, combine the basil, oil, Parmesan, broth, lemon juice, garlic, pepper, and salt. Purée the mixture for 45 seconds. Marinate meat or poultry for 2 hours to overnight; shrimp for up to 1 hour. (If marinating for more than 1 hour, cover and refrigerate.)

KITCHEN NOTE: *More commonly used on pasta, this basil preparation adds punch to grilled chicken (especially skinned thighs), pork cutlets or chops, and shrimp. Don't use all the pesto as a marinade; reserve a little to serve at the table. This recipe makes enough for 2 to 3 pounds meat, poultry, or shrimp.*

RED WINE AND
BAY LEAF MARINADE

SERVES 6 TO 8

🕐 EXTRA-QUICK

¾ CUP DRY RED WINE

¼ CUP OLIVE OIL

2 TABLESPOONS RED WINE VINEGAR

3 GARLIC CLOVES, MINCED

4 BAY LEAVES

¾ TEASPOON SALT

¼ TEASPOON BLACK PEPPER

½ TEASPOON THYME

1. In a medium bowl, combine the wine, oil, vinegar, garlic, bay leaves, salt, pepper, and thyme. Marinate meat for at least 2 hours and up to 8 hours. (If marinating for more than 1 hour, cover and refrigerate.)

KITCHEN NOTE: *This marinade adds plenty of flavor to red meat and is especially good on less expensive cuts such as chuck steak. Baste the meat with the marinade as it cooks and for best flavor, cook the meat rare and slice it thin.*

Soy Sauce and Ginger Marinade

S E R V E S   6   T O   8

🕐 E X T R A - Q U I C K

½ CUP REDUCED-SODIUM SOY SAUCE

3 TABLESPOONS LIGHT BROWN SUGAR

3 TABLESPOONS KETCHUP

1 TABLESPOON ORIENTAL (DARK)
    SESAME OIL

2 TABLESPOONS DRY WHITE WINE

1 TABLESPOON GRATED FRESH GINGER

1 TO 2 TEASPOONS MINCED FRESH
    JALAPEÑO PEPPER

1. In a medium bowl, combine the soy sauce, brown sugar, ketchup, oil, wine, ginger, and jalapeño pepper. Marinate chicken or meat for at least 2 hours, or overnight; fish for 1 hour. (If marinating for more than 1 hour, cover and refrigerate.)

KITCHEN NOTE: *This recipe makes enough for a whole cut-up chicken, or 2 to 3 pounds of pork chops, pork tenderloin, or fish fillets. Grill on a medium flame, or broil 6 inches from the heat and turn the food often, as the sauce has a tendency to scorch.*

White Wine and Rosemary Marinade

SERVES 6 TO 8

⏱ EXTRA-QUICK

1 CUP DRY WHITE WINE

¾ CUP THINLY SLICED SHALLOT OR
ONION

⅓ CUP OLIVE OIL

1 TABLESPOON PLUS 2 TEASPOONS
CHOPPED FRESH ROSEMARY LEAVES,
OR 2 TEASPOONS DRIED

ONE 2-INCH STRIP LEMON ZEST

1 TABLESPOON BALSAMIC VINEGAR

2 GARLIC CLOVES, LIGHTLY CRUSHED

½ TEASPOON SALT

½ TEASPOON BLACK PEPPER

1. In a medium bowl, combine the wine, shallot or onion, the oil, rosemary, lemon zest, vinegar, garlic, salt, and pepper. Marinate chicken, veal, or vegetables for up to 3 hours. (If marinating for more than 1 hour, cover and refrigerate.)

Kitchen Note: *This recipe makes enough for 2 to 3 pounds chicken, veal, or vegetables. Baste with the marinade while grilling, and for extra flavor and aroma, add a few rosemary sprigs to the coals.*

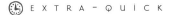
Tomato-Molasses Barbecue Sauce

SERVES 16

⏱ EXTRA-QUICK

2 TABLESPOONS BUTTER

½ CUP CHOPPED ONION

½ CUP DICED GREEN BELL PEPPER

2 GARLIC CLOVES, MINCED

1 BAY LEAF

¼ TEASPOON GROUND CLOVES

ONE 28-OUNCE CAN TOMATOES, DRAINED AND PURÉED IN FOOD PROCESSOR

1 CUP KETCHUP

ONE 6-OUNCE CAN TOMATO PASTE

¼ CUP CIDER VINEGAR

¼ CUP MOLASSES

1 TABLESPOON YELLOW MUSTARD

1 TEASPOON HOT PEPPER SAUCE

½ TEASPOON SALT

1. In a large nonstick saucepan, warm the butter over medium heat until melted. Add the onion, bell pepper, garlic, bay leaf, and cloves and sauté for 5 minutes, stirring frequently, until the vegetables are tender.

2. Stir in the puréed tomatoes, the ketchup, 1 cup of water, tomato paste, vinegar, molasses, mustard, hot pepper sauce, and salt and bring to a boil. Reduce the heat to low, cover and simmer for 40 minutes, stirring occasionally, until the sauce is thickened. Serve hot or cold.

KITCHEN NOTE: *This basic sauce is the one everyone is sure to love, on ribs, burgers, steaks, chicken, or shrimp. Brush the sauce on only during the last 5 to 10 minutes of cooking, or it will burn. Serve extra sauce at the table for dipping. This recipe makes a big batch but you can halve the recipe, if you prefer. It keeps for weeks in the refrigerator.*

VINEGARY BARBECUE BRUSHING SAUCE

SERVES 8

⊕ EXTRA-QUICK

1 STICK UNSALTED BUTTER

1 GARLIC CLOVE, LIGHTLY CRUSHED

¼ CUP PLUS 3 TABLESPOONS CIDER
  VINEGAR

¾ TEASPOON SALT

1 TEASPOON BLACK PEPPER

½ TEASPOON RED PEPPER FLAKES

1. In a small saucepan, warm the butter with the garlic over low heat until the butter is melted. Add the vinegar, salt, pepper, and red pepper flakes. Increase the heat slightly and bring to a boil. Reduce the heat to low and simmer for 10 minutes.

KITCHEN NOTE: *This lively baste is enough for 2 to 4 pounds of chicken, turkey, or pork cutlets. Spoon it on both sides of whatever you're cooking, and baste when you turn for a peppery, intense flavor. This baste doesn't work well with skin-on chicken because the flavor won't penetrate the skin.*

Guacamole

SERVES 8

🕐 EXTRA-QUICK

2 MEDIUM AVOCADOS

1 CUP DICED TOMATO

¼ CUP MINCED WHITE OR RED ONION

2 TABLESPOONS FRESH LIME JUICE

½ TEASPOON CUMIN

¼ TEASPOON SALT

FEW DROPS HOT PEPPER SAUCE, TO
  TASTE

1. Cut the avocados in half lengthwise and remove the pits. Place the halves in a large bowl and mash with a potato masher or fork.

2. Add the tomato, onion, lime juice, cumin, salt, and hot pepper sauce and stir to blend. Serve immediately.

Kitchen Note: *Serve the guacamole on turkey or beef burgers, with grilled chicken or steak. It's great with grilled tortillas, too. Guacamole tastes best when freshly made.*

CREAMY HONEY-MUSTARD SAUCE

SERVES 8

EXTRA-QUICK

¼ CUP PLAIN NONFAT YOGURT

¼ CUP SOUR CREAM

2 TABLESPOONS HONEY

1 TABLESPOON DIJON MUSTARD

1 TABLESPOON GRAINY MUSTARD

1 TABLESPOON THINLY SLICED
  SCALLION GREENS

⅛ TEASPOON BLACK PEPPER

1. In a medium bowl, mix the yogurt, sour cream, honey, mustards, scallion greens, and pepper until well blended. The sauce will keep in the refrigerator up to 4 days.

KITCHEN NOTE: *Serve this sauce with grilled shrimp, grilled swordfish, or pork chops. It also makes a luscious low-calorie dip for crisp veggies.*

Pineapple-Red Pepper Relish

SERVES 8

⏱ EXTRA-QUICK ♡ LOW-FAT

1½ CUPS FINELY DICED FRESH OR
    DRAINED JUICE-PACKED CANNED
    PINEAPPLE
1 MEDIUM RED BELL PEPPER, FINELY
    DICED
2 TABLESPOONS MINCED RED ONION

1 TABLESPOON CHOPPED PARSLEY
2 TEASPOONS SUGAR
2 TEASPOONS RED WINE VINEGAR
¼ TEASPOON SALT
⅛ TEASPOON BLACK PEPPER
⅛ TEASPOON RED PEPPER FLAKES

1. In a medium bowl, stir together the pineapple, bell pepper, onion, parsley, sugar, vinegar, salt, black pepper, and red pepper flakes until blended. Cover and chill for at least 30 minutes before serving. The relish will keep 1 to 2 days in the refrigerator.

Kitchen Note: *Look for peeled and cored fresh pineapple in the produce section of your supermarket. Serve this refreshing and colorful relish alongside grilled chicken or turkey breasts, or with grilled pork cutlets or sea scallops.*

PLUM AND RAISIN CHUTNEY

SERVES 8

🕐 EXTRA-QUICK

1 TABLESPOON OLIVE OIL

⅓ CUP CHOPPED RED ONION

1 GARLIC CLOVE, MINCED

½ TEASPOON GROUND GINGER

⅛ TEASPOON ALLSPICE

3 TABLESPOONS LIGHT BROWN SUGAR

1 POUND FRESH PLUMS, DICED

⅓ CUP GOLDEN RAISINS

2 TABLESPOONS BALSAMIC VINEGAR

1. In a medium nonstick saucepan, warm the oil over medium heat. Add the onion, garlic, ginger, and allspice and sauté for 3 to 4 minutes, stirring frequently, until onion is tender.

2. Add the sugar and stir until it melts. Stir in the plums and raisins and bring to a simmer. Reduce the heat to medium-low, cover and simmer for 5 to 7 minutes, stirring occasionally, until the plums are tender and translucent but not mushy.

3. Add the vinegar and let boil, uncovered, for 1 minute. Refrigerate for at least 1 day before serving. The chutney will keep up to 1 week in the refrigerator.

KITCHEN NOTE: *This chutney is lovely on grilled turkey, or lamb chops, or chicken. Be sure to make it the day before serving it so the flavors can blend and mellow.*

SALSA CRUDA

SERVES 8

⏱ EXTRA-QUICK   ♡ LOW-FAT

2 TEASPOONS CUMIN

3 CUPS DICED TOMATOES

⅓ CUP CHOPPED FRESH CILANTRO,
INCLUDING SOME OF THE STEMS

¼ CUP DICED RED ONION

2 TABLESPOONS FRESH LIME JUICE

1 TABLESPOON MINCED PICKLED
JALAPEÑO PEPPER

½ TEASPOON SALT

1. Put the cumin in a small nonstick skillet and cook over medium-high heat, stirring frequently, until fragrant and the color darkens slightly, about 3 minutes. Remove from the heat and immediately tip into a medium bowl.

2. Add the tomatoes, cilantro, onion, lime juice, jalapeño pepper, and salt to the cumin and stir to mix. Cover and let stand 30 minutes at room temperature to blend the flavors before serving.

KITCHEN NOTE: *Serve on burgers, grilled steak or chops, or plain fish fillets, or with a big bowl of tortilla chips.*

Dilled Lemon-Yogurt Sauce

SERVES 8

⏰ EXTRA-QUICK

½ CUP PLAIN LOW-FAT YOGURT

½ CUP SOUR CREAM

3 TABLESPOONS FRESH LEMON JUICE

2 TABLESPOONS MINCED DILL PICKLE

2 TABLESPOONS MINCED FRESH DILL

½ TEASPOON SALT

½ TEASPOON DRAINED CAPERS

¼ TEASPOON BLACK PEPPER

1. In a medium bowl, whisk together the yogurt, sour cream, lemon juice, dill pickle, dill, salt, capers, and pepper until well blended.

2. Cover and chill at least 30 minutes so the flavors can blend. This sauce will keep up to 3 days in the refrigerator.

Kitchen Note: *A perfect sauce for grilled fish steaks (halibut and salmon are especially good), also grilled shrimp or scallops. Leftover sauce is good with canned tuna or as a dip for carrot sticks.*

FRESH SPICY TOMATO SAUCE

SERVES 8

⏱ EXTRA-QUICK

1 TABLESPOON OLIVE OIL
¼ CUP CHOPPED ONION
¼ CUP DICED RED BELL PEPPER
2 GARLIC CLOVES, MINCED
¼ TEASPOON BASIL

¼ TEASPOON SALT
⅛ TEASPOON BLACK PEPPER
⅛ TEASPOON RED PEPPER FLAKES
1 POUND TOMATOES, PEELED AND CUT
   INTO CHUNKS

I. In a medium nonstick saucepan, warm the oil over medium-high heat. Add the onion, bell pepper, garlic, basil, salt, black pepper, and red pepper flakes and sauté for 3 to 4 minutes, stirring frequently, until the vegetables are tender.

2. Stir in the tomatoes, increase the heat to high, and cook, stirring frequently, until the juices start to flow and the tomatoes begin to collapse, about 5 minutes.

3. Reduce the heat to medium-low and simmer the sauce for 20 minutes, or until the tomatoes have cooked down and the sauce is slightly thickened. Serve hot. Keeps up to 4 days in the refrigerator.

KITCHEN NOTE: *Serve over grilled swordfish and scallop skewers or with veal chops, grilled vegetables, or even a plain burger.*

İnDEX

Recipes that are marked in the body of the book with the symbol ☺ take 45 minutes or less to prepare. They are grouped in the index under the name Extra-Quick. Recipes that are marked in the body of the book with the symbol ♡ derive 30% or fewer of their calories from fat. They are grouped in the index under the name Low-Fat.